Hitler's Motorcars

Hitler's Motorcars

The Führer's Vehicles From the Birth of the Nazi Party to the Fall of the Third Reich

John Starkey

Frontline Books

First published in Great Britain in 2023 by
Frontline Books
An imprint of Pen & Sword Books Limited
Yorkshire – Philadelphia

ISBN 978 1 39907 141 3

A CIP catalogue record for this book is
available from the British Library

Typeset by Mac Style
Printed in the UK by CPI Group (UK) Ltd, Croydon, CR0 4YY.

MIX
Paper | Supporting
responsible forestry
FSC® C013604

Pen & Sword Books Limited incorporates the imprints of After the Battle,
Atlas, Archaeology, Aviation, Discovery, Family History, Fiction, History,
Maritime, Military, Military Classics, Politics, Select, Transport, True Crime,
Air World, Frontline Publishing, Leo Cooper, Remember When, Seaforth
Publishing, The Praetorian Press, Wharncliffe Local History, Wharncliffe
Transport, Wharncliffe True Crime and White Owl.

For a complete list of Pen & Sword titles please contact

PEN & SWORD BOOKS LIMITED
47 Church Street, Barnsley, South Yorkshire, S70 2AS, England
E-mail: enquiries@pen-and-sword.co.uk
Website: www.pen-and-sword.co.uk
or
PEN AND SWORD BOOKS
1950 Lawrence Rd, Havertown, PA 19083, USA
E-mail: Uspen-and-sword@casematepublishers.com
Website: www.penandswordbooks.com

Contents

Preface

Hitler transformed Germany after he came to power on 30 January 1933. Before that, Germany had been struggling, economy wise, government wise, and socially. Hitler issued draconian decrees to bring all this under control and to expand Germany in every way, in order to fulfil his desire of seeing, once again, a great Germany that had, in his opinion, been forced to its knees by the Treaty of Versailles, which signified the end of the First World War.

Hitler hated that treaty. Apart from anything else, such as the enormous financial reparations demanded, it also took away parts of the country that Hitler saw as rightfully belonging to Germany and he vowed to get them back. By 1939, he had.

In 1969, the test pilot Captain Eric Brown wrote in his book *Wings of the Luftwaffe* (McDonald and Jane's, 1977) about testing various German aircraft of the Second World War. He had spent a lot of time in his youth living in Germany in the 1930s and, in the foreword he wrote:

> I was to return to Germany to continue my studies in the environment of the third Reich and acquired my pilot's wings. Much has been written of the evils of this era in Germany, but to a young and impressionable foreigner the atmosphere was one of vibrant excitement and military pageantry. I was too inexperienced to sense the underlying tensions and above all I was bewitched by the tremendous aviation activity throughout the country.
>
> There seemed to be many more powerful aircraft and gliders than I had ever seen in England, and the youth of Germany was being encouraged to participate in the sport of aviation at no personal expense. To me, it seemed truly an aviator's Utopia.

Hitler not only encouraged the youth of Germany to learn to fly, he provided the same encouragement to all young people to learn to drive. A whole generation of German youth was being prepared to operate aircraft, trucks and cars, so if war came they would be prepared for a new, mechanised type of warfare.

Hitler loved cars. Yes, he could drive but he hardly ever bothered, as from 1921 onwards he always had a series of willing chauffeurs to drive him around in a series of virtually the best German cars that money could buy. This was particularly the case from 1926, when he started receiving the royalties from *Mein Kampf*, which sold in the millions and made Hitler a millionaire.

This then is the story of the cars that Hitler used in his rise to be the dictator of Germany.

Introduction

Adolf Hitler was fascinated by cars. So much so that, according to him, he discussed many new body designs with the management of Mercedes-Benz in the mid to late 1930s. He certainly sketched out the shape of the Volkswagen Beetle. That sketch still exists.

Whenever the subject of Hitler arises, many people turn away. He was one of the major figures of the twentieth century and some of his actions have seen him labelled as a monster.

This book is about a subject related to him that is hardly ever raised: the motor cars that he travelled in. I say 'travelled in' because he was always photographed as the passenger; standing on a special platform in the front passenger compartment, waving to the adoring, saluting crowds as he passed by.

Hitler was very interested in technical matters. He took a great interest in anything mechanical, visiting the Berlin Motor Show every year when it opened and looking at every new technical development, both at that show and also what was taking place in industry in Germany during his time as Chancellor.

His government's sponsoring of Mercedes and Auto Union Grand Prix race cars is well known, as he saw it as a way to showcase Germany's technical excellence but that subject has been very well covered elsewhere and is not a part of this book.

Apart from the Selve cars that Hitler started the 1920s with, he was always later on seen in a Benz, or a Mercedes-Benz. He admired the design and workmanship of them; it is a little-known fact that he was involved in two accidents while being driven, both times in Mercedes-Benz cars. He escaped both with only a broken finger and bruises from one. This led him to tell his friends that he would never ride in any other car except for a Mercedes-Benz.

What is often not realised is that by 1926–27 Hitler was a very wealthy man. He could afford to buy any car that he liked. *Mein Kampf*, written in 1924 while he was confined in Landsberg prison, sold in the millions and gave him the money that he could use to buy whatever he wanted. He also solely owned the *Völkischer Beobachter*, the daily newspaper of the Nazi Party, which sometimes sold up to 1.7 million copies a day.

The Nazi Party, led by Adolf Hitler, staged what had to be the largest, most imposing rallies that the world had ever seen until after the Second World War at their parade ground at Nuremburg. Perhaps it was inevitable that the vehicles that Hitler travelled in were also unparalleled for their sheer size and grandeur as well. During the 1930s, Hitler was nearly always to be seen in either a Grosser (Great) Mercedes-Benz W07/W150, or a G-4 six-wheeled vehicle, intended for cross-country trips.

Here, then, is the story of Hitler's cars. As I write in September 2022, there are still a couple of small mysteries about exactly which car did what, but we shall get to them …

Acknowledgements

First of all to my friend and colleague Franco Varani, who, true to form and despite telling me that he 'didn't know much about old cars …' immediately pointed out that in the only two photographs of Hitler in 1920s' Selve cars, the door-shut lines of one were different to the other, therefore showing that these photos were of two different cars. Well done Franco.

Secondly to my publisher, John Grehan of Pen and Sword who, out of the blue, commissioned me to write this book, saying: 'You're our car guy, so you can write this!' after telling me that his partner, Martin Mace, had many photographs of Hitler in various different cars in his career and could I write the words for a book that would feature these photos.

I should like to be able to thank the Mercedes Archives. Unfortunately, whilst being unfailingly polite in our email exchanges, they informed me that the powers that be there, (whoever they are), have decided that they wish to draw a veil over the time that Hitler was in power in Germany and not give out any details of the many Mercedes that he and his colleagues rode in. The Second World War ended over seventy-six years ago as I write. It's time to study history with a dispassionate eye now.

Dieter Dressel of the Mercedes Kompressor Klub E.V. was very helpful in trying to trace what had happened with some of the 'Grosser' Mercedes 770Ks and Kevin Wheatcroft gave great help detailing the W150 770K that his collection owns. Likewise, the Canadian War Museum in Ottawa was very helpful in detailing the car it has on display.

Among the research that I conducted in writing this book, I was greatly helped by the photographs in the books of Jan Melin and Blaine Taylor, so a big thank you to both, particularly to Jan, whose two volumes on the eight-cylinder supercharged Mercedes-Benz are a must for any serious enthusiasts of these cars of the 1930s and early '40s.

And, of course, many thanks to my wife Su, who has had to listen to me going on about exactly which cars belonged to Hitler, or the government of Germany during his career. Thanks Su, you're a star.

Chapter 1

Hitler's Early Life and Cars, 1889–1921

There he stands, lips set in a grim, no-nonsense line under his toothbrush moustache. Like some Roman Emperor of old, he acknowledges the salutes and roars of approval from the adoring crowd as he passes by, with his backhanded acknowledgement of their cries of 'Sieg Heil!'[1]

A Roman emperor of old would have stood in a gold-plated chariot but Hitler's chariot is a chrome-plated Grosser Mercedes, and he has not four, but two hundred and thirty horses to propel him.

In the old black and white photographs of him, we can clearly see that Hitler, in his customary uniform jacket, or, if the weather is perverse, his long black leather raincoat, is standing on a special platform built into the passenger seat of his open Mercedes-Benz open touring car. This allows him to see and be seen, as he waves his careless offhand right-handed salute to the crowd. Alongside him, his black cap clearly showing the skull and crossed bones badge of the SS, is his chauffeur, usually, particularly in the latter years of the Reich, the imperturbable Sturmbahnnführer Erich Kempka.[2]

Hitler loved parades. The bigger the cars, the more of them in the parade itself, the better. Just where did this leader of Germany, der Führer, originate?

Hitler had come from a middle class background. His father, Alois Schicklgruber, was illegitimate and he later on changed his name to Alois Hitler. That may have been the name of his real father. Alois was a customs official, a bureaucrat. Young Adolf had been born in a house in Braunau am Inn, near to Linz, Austria, in 1889. In 1892 the family moved to Passau, in Bavaria, Southern Germany. Two years later the family was back in Austria, in Leonding. A year later saw another move, to Hafeld, near to Lambach.

School at Fischlham beckoned but there were, apparently, 'disciplinary problems' which involved young Adolf, his father and the school. In 1897, Adolf is noted as having sung in a choir in Lambach before moving back to Leonding in 1899. Two years later, Hitler was at 'Realschule' in Linz, Austria, before moving school yet again in 1904 to Steyr, again in Austria. At the age of sixteen, he left school.

Hitler wanted to be an artist and in 1908 he moved to Vienna in order to take the entrance examination of the Vienna Academy of the Arts, but he failed it. Hitler's mother, who he loved dearly, died of breast cancer in the same year and by 1909, after going through the money that his mother had left him, he was reduced to being a casual labourer, sleeping in homeless shelters or men's dormitories in the Mariahilf district. To earn some extra money, he would paint and sell watercolours, helped by a friend who acted as his agent, one Reinhold Hanisch.[3]

By 1913, Hitler's father had also died and Adolf received part of his father's estate. More importantly where Hitler's finances were concerned, his aunt Johanna in 1910 bequeathed him his inheritance, from her, of 2,000 crowns.[4]

On 13 May 1913, Hitler received orders from the Austrian military authorities to attend a medical examination prior to being drafted into the Austrian army to serve his compulsory military service. This was not something that Hitler wanted to do, if he was going to serve in any army, it would, by his choice, be the German army. He moved to Munich in Bavaria, Germany, on 24 May, in an attempt to escape this but the Austrian authorities tracked him down and on 18 January 1914 he was arrested in Munich, held in jail overnight and was in court the next day.

There he pleaded an inability to serve in the Austrian army due to frostbite that he had suffered while a labourer in Vienna. He was instructed to attend a medical examination at Salzburg on 5 February. The verdict of the doctor was: 'Unfit for general and limited service; too weak. Graded as F-4.'

Back in Munich, Hitler carried on with his painting until 3 August 1914. Then, he can be clearly seen in a photograph, taken by Heinrich Hoffman (later on to become Hitler's official photographer from 1922), among the crowd that had gathered in front of the city hall that day. That crowd was wildly cheering on the announcement of the outbreak of the First World War. Hitler enlisted in the Bavarian army, and on 16 August he joined the 6th Recruit Replacement Battalion of the 2nd Bavarian Infantry Regiment, number 16 (The List Regiment), after apparently petitioning King Ludwig III of Bavaria for permission for him to do so. Hitler was an Austrian by birth but was accepted into the German army.

Germany, as a country, was only forty-three years old in 1914. She had been formed by the actions of Otto von Bismarck, chief adviser to King Wilhelm of Prussia, in 1870, Prussia being the main state from which military officers and the estate-owning Junkers came. The other kingdoms, principalities, duchies and grand duchies that made up the new Germany numbered twenty-five, including Bavaria, Saxony and Württemberg, to name some of the largest. In 1871, the new Germany had promptly gone to war with France and defeated it, absorbing Alsace-Lorraine as one of its spoils.

Hitler and his regiment were shipped to the Western Front in October 1914, after inadequate training. They took part in the murderous First Battle of Ypres in 1914. After this, Hitler was awarded the Iron Cross, second class, for his actions. He was also at the Battle of the Somme in 1916, where he was wounded by a shell fragment in his left thigh. Then he was present at the Battle of Arras in 1916 and at the Battle of Passchendaele in 1917. For most of the time, Hitler was a regimental runner, meaning that he took messages from the regiment's headquarters, in Fournes-en-Weppes, a town in northern France far from the front-line trenches, to battalion headquarters, all behind the trench lines. He did not fight in the trenches. Nevertheless, Hitler was also awarded the Iron Cross, first class, on 4 August 1918. But he was only ever promoted to be a gefreiter, loosely equivalent to a squad leader/ lance corporal, not having even been promoted to full corporal.

On 8 October 1918, Hitler was blinded in a British mustard gas attack in Belgium and hospitalised. Whilst in hospital, he learned of Germany's defeat and the acceptance of an armistice, signed on 11 November 1918. This news led to him suffering a second bout of blindness, this time psychosomatic. One doctor classified him as 'a psychopath, with hysterical tendencies'. On 21 November, he was discharged from the Pasewalk Military Reserve Hospital, near to Stettin, and some days later he was back in Munich, still attached to the List Regiment, stationed at the Max II barracks on Oberwiesen Field.

By this time, the King of Bavaria had been deposed and Bavaria was now governed by a left-wing government, led by Kurt Eisner. Eisner was assassinated on 21 February 1919, by Count Anton Arco auf Valley, a former 2nd lieutenant in the German army with right-wing sympathies.[5]

Hitler and a few other men of his unit walked behind the coffin at Eisner's funeral to show their respect. Hitler wore the black armband of mourning, but also the red armband of the socialist revolution that was about to take place in Munich. On 6 April, the Socialist Republic of Bavaria was proclaimed and Hitler was elected as a deputy battalion representative, liaising with the Department of Propaganda.

There is a reported story that during this time (February 1919), Hitler and another soldier were attacked by some 200 others after Hitler gave a speech in a gymnasium. A German-speaking Irishman, Michael Keogh, who was fighting with the Freikorps at the time, later reported that he and seven other men had broken up the fight and that: 'The fellow with the moustache gave his name promptly: Adolf Hitler.' We have no way of corroborating this story but it was reported in later years in Irish newspapers.[6]

The Bavarian Soviet Republic, a rival of the Socialist Republic, was put down by the Freikorps, who were a volunteer militia, mainly ex-army soldiers who re-joined the army to help put down left-wing insurrections. During the first week of May, some 606 people, both soldiers and civilians, were killed. Over 1,000 people were later tried and executed and the attempted communist domination of Bavaria was averted.

Hitler's role in this mini revolution was shadowy but he probably informed his commanding officers as to who were the main leaders of the proclaimed Soviet

Republic. While no proof has ever emerged, it seems likely that Hitler was acting as a double agent at this time, with his true allegiance being to the officers of the army, who commanded him and who were opposed to the new republic. It may have been at this juncture that Hitler's hatred of communism, particularly Bolshevism, began. At this time, although a mere corporal, Hitler had an expense account and was allowed to wear civilian clothes. He had obviously impressed his superiors with his ability in gathering intelligence.

During the First World War, Hitler had never shown any signs of being anti-Semitic; indeed, there were several Jews in the List Regiment and there were no reports of them being treated badly by their comrades. It seems probable that Hitler, casting about after Germany's defeat for a culprit, saw the people who financed the war, many of them being Jews, as the people responsible for Germany's humiliation. In Southern Germany and Austria, there had long been a history of anti-Semitism. This, coupled with Hitler's unfailing respect for the mainly right-leaning officers who commanded him during and after the war, led to his anti-Semitic and anti-communist leanings. These thoughts manifested themselves in his speeches of later years.

After this, Hitler remained in the army, being appointed as an intelligence/propaganda agent of a reconnaissance unit in July 1919 under a Hauptmann (Captain) Karl Mayr. Hitler was sent by Mayr and his military intelligence superiors to anti-communist training courses and university seminars, which were financed by the military administration and the Thule Society. There are many rumours that this society was based on black magic and, certainly, the rituals and parades of the Nazi Party seem to show a love of ritual.

With his work on intelligence matters while in the army, Hitler had learned that the DAP, (Deutsche Arbeiterpartei, German Workers' Party) was also funded by the Thule Society, which had been formed in 1912. This was a lodge, based on Freemasonry and named the Order of Teutons. Its members were anti-Semitic and anti-Marxist, and several of them were also in positions of power and influence and some were very rich. A certain Rudolf Hess, later to become Hitler's secretary, was a very active organiser for them. It was at this time that Hitler met many influential scholars and politicians, who were to come to his party's help in the future.

Hitler, in his everyday work, gave talks about politics to soldiers and then, on 12 September 1919, and now a private first class in section Ib/P 4th Bavarian Reichswehr 'Armed Forces' Group HQ, he was assigned by Hauptmann Mayr to investigate the small DAP in Munich.[7]

The DAP had been formed on 5 January 1919 by Anton Drexler, with Dietrich Eckart, Karl Harrer and Gottfried Feder. Harrer was a member of the Thule Society, as were many early members of the DAP.

Hitler was so impressed by the DAP that he joined it, apparently on the orders of his army superiors. He was member number 555 – membership started with number 500 – and, on 12 September 1919, Hitler gave his first speech in public in the Leiber Room of the Sternecker beer hall in Munich. The main speaker that night was engineer Gottfried Feder, who talked about how Jews controlled lending capital. Feder was also a member of the Thule Society.

Straight away, Hitler impressed other people in his party with his passionate speech delivery and the fact that he had got into an argument with a Professor Baumann that same night, who was not impressed by Feder's arguments. Hitler soon argued him down, until Baumann left the meeting, and Hitler quickly became his new party's most prominent speaker. In particular, the party chairman, one Anton Drexler, was sufficiently impressed by Hitler's speech-making ability that he encouraged him by giving him *My Political Awakening*, a pamphlet he had written. Drexler's particular brand of politics was a mixture of anti-Marxism, anti-communism, anti-Semitism, and strident German nationalism.[8]

Towards the end of 1919, Hitler met Dietrich Eckart. The DAP had been co-founded by Eckart, an anti-Semitic playwright and activist. Eckart became Hitler's mentor, teaching him how to speak better, improving his table manners and etiquette, plus introducing Hitler to wealthy patrons of the Munich arts scene, particularly the anti-Semites.

Subsequently, Hitler's reputation as a fiery orator grew and in February 1920 he gave a speech to over 2,000 people. His speeches featured diatribes against the Treaty of Versailles (which ratified the end of the First World War in June, 1919), Marxists (Hitler by now hated communism, particularly after the Bavarian uprising), the Weimar Government, and Jews. In these points, his views closely echoed those of Drexler.

The DAP was renamed the Nationalsozialistische Deutsche Arbeiterpartei (NSDAP, or Nazi) on 24 February 1920 and Hitler is reputed to have designed the flag of a swastika on a white circle against a red background himself. The flag itself was reputedly made by Jenny Haug, Hitler's girlfriend at the time.

Jenny was a member of the NSDAP from March 1920. Her brother, Ernst, became Hitler's first, of several, chauffeurs. Hitler is reported to have parted from Jenny when she showed him a small revolver that she said that she had bought to protect him in one of the many fights between the Nazis and communists that frequently broke out in local beer halls when Hitler made his speeches. However, this may be apocryphal as Jenny remained a member of the Nazi Party until at least 1935.[9]

In March 1920, Dietrich Eckart and Hitler, in civilian clothes, travelled to Berlin by aircraft from Munich to contact the leaders of a right-wing coup that had taken place there. The aircraft became lost and landed 70km south of Berlin, at Jüterbog. There they were interrogated by officials of the ousted Social Democrat government. Eckart told his interrogators that he was a businessman from Munich, and that Hitler was his bookkeeper. They were able to travel on to Berlin but by the time they arrived there, the coup had collapsed. Had their real identity been revealed, they probably would have been executed.

While in Berlin on this occasion, Eckart introduced Hitler to General Erich Ludendorff, who had been, after Hindenburg, the second highest-ranking German officer in the war just finished. Apparently Hitler acted in a very servile manner towards Ludendorff.[10]

On 31 March 1920, Hitler was demobilised from the German army. He had been receiving his army pay of 20 gold marks a week up until now. During this time, he had stayed at his friend Hans Mend's apartment and had visited his old army comrade Josef Inkofer several times.[11]

One of Hitler's most important aims that he emphasised in his early speeches was to take back those territories that the Allies had taken from Germany at the end of the war: Austria, Czechoslovakia and the new Poland …

With money being donated to the Nazi Party, particularly from his new wealthy friends, Hitler was able to buy a car in 1920, a second-hand 1920 light green Selve 6/20, sometimes referred to as a '20CV', with a side valve four-cylinder engine of 1.5 litres, driving the rear wheels via a four-speed gearbox. This was the car that Hitler's friend 'Putzi' Hanfstaengl would refer to as 'the Rattling Monster'. Apparently, Hitler bought it with money that 'he had drummed up in a mysterious way from someone'.

That 'someone' was the party funds. According to Wulf Schwarzweiler, in his book *The Unknown Hitler* (National Press and Star Agency, 1989):

> In the summer of 1920, Hitler was obsessed with the idea of getting a car. He frequently showed up in the salesrooms of car dealers and looked at the models. One Monday evening in the Cafe Neumaier, he informed his speechless party members that they'd have to buy him a car so that he could get to meetings faster. A car would give him – and the party – a certain amount of dignity and put them above the Marxists who walked or took the streetcar. Somehow Hitler managed to rebut all the arguments and the party scraped the money together.

The Selve car-making company was based in Hamelin, of Pied Piper fame. It was headed by Walther von Selve, scion of a family of industrialists. Among other companies, they owned and ran a metal works in Altena in Westphalia, one of the best in Germany. Walther, who was born in 1876, had raced motorbikes, speedboats and cars before 1900.

The Selve V-shaped radiator. (*Photo courtesy of the Claus H. Wulff Emblem Collection*)

Acceding to become the head of the family business in 1911, he knew that among his family's companies was the Basse & Selve engine building factory, also in Altena. During the war, this company had built straight six engines, modelled on the Mercedes and Benz 260hp aero engines. Selve also owned, at this time, 1919, the Northern German Automobile Works (Norddeutsche Automobilwerke). They also made the Sperber and Colibri cars. The chief designer of the Selve car company was ex-Daimler and Imperia engineer Ernst Lehmann.

In 1920 there was a totally new range of Selve cars, the 6/24, 8/30 (later the 8/32), and the 8/40 sports car. The first production vehicles with four-cylinder engines were fitted with aluminium pistons, a Selve invention dating back to 1921, although W.O. Bentley had used aluminium pistons both in his first cars, copying the French DFP car, and in his excellent Bentley rotary engines that powered such aircraft as the Sopwith Camel and Snipe.

The Selve cars had sporting pretensions; in 1921, they came first and second (in class) in May at 'the Opel race' and finished in the top three positions in class at Ruselberg in September and then, in October, at the Reichsfahrt meeting, they finished first and second. In 1922, although the factory did not enter any of their cars, private entrants did finish in first and third places in class at the Reichsfahrt, which was probably in a hill climb.

Tragically, in 1924 technical director Ernst Lehmann was killed in an accident during practice at the Teutoburg Forest Race. He was replaced by Karl Slevogt, one of the more prominent designers of the time.

Interestingly, in 1928, the Selve company produced the Selve M, using three axles and six wheels (shades of the Mercedes-Benz G4 that Hitler would later use so often). It was intended to be sold to the Wehrmacht but at this time they did not foresee a use for motorised infantry. Production of Selve cars halted in 1929 due to the financial crash and the company finally closed in 1934.[12]

Hanfstaengl reported:

Selve Oldtimer 1921 Advertisement. (*Photo courtesy of the Claus H. Wulff Emblem Collection*)

> At this period, (Hitler), would often be discovered in a salesroom looking at second-hand automobiles. Cars were an obsession with him. He picked up one vehicle which looked like a dismantled horse-cab without a top, but soon exchanged this for another Selve car, with funds he had drummed up in a mysterious way from someone. It was a rattling monster and each end looked as if it were going a different way, but he seemed to think it conferred additional dignity on him and from that time on I do not think I ever saw him take a tram or bus again.[13]

Wulf Schwarzwaller wrote:

> The party treasury scraped the money together for a vehicle that looked 'like a horse-drawn coach without a roof.' At first Hitler, who'd learned how to drive while in the army, drove the car himself, but it broke down so often that he became disenchanted with it. He returned the pre-historic car to the party and, with his own money, purchased another used 'Selve', probably the new car did not look much better than the old one, but it was in better shape. From then on, Hitler was never again seen getting into a streetcar on a bus.[14]

The 'used Selve' that Schwarzwaller referred to was probably the more powerful 32hp, 2-litre car, still with four cylinders.

RIR 16, Hitler's old regiment, had had a staff sergeant called Max Amann. In May 1921, Hitler persuaded his old comrade to become the managing director of the new NSDAP, and to bring the organisational qualities that he had displayed at Regimental Headquarters of the List Regiment with him. By 1922, Amann was the managing director of the Franz Eher publishing house, the publisher of the Nazi newspaper, the *Völkischer Beobachter*. This would lead to Amann becoming a very wealthy man and he survived the Second World War, being captured later on and interrogated by the American forces.[15]

July 1921 saw Hitler become the chairman of the Nazi Party and he made the decision that the headquarters should stay in Munich. On 29 July, this decision was passed by a vote of 533 to 1. Hitler's tremendous appeal spread throughout Germany by word of mouth, mainly due to his talent as a speech-maker. He vilified all who did not agree with him and his party, and had his supporters take part in hand-to-hand brawls against their Jewish and communist opponents.

Hitler mastered the art of speech-making in these early years of the Nazi Party. He saw how well his hatred of the loss of the First World War, the Treaty of Versailles that signified its end, the Jews and the profiteers of the war went down with his audience, and he also saw the value of symbols for his new party.

Apart from the flag featuring the swastika, he also had former army Hauptmann (Captain) Ernst Röhm form a bodyguard, the Sturmabteilung (Storm Detachment), usually shortened to 'SA', on 5 October 1921. These were paramilitary troops, who were financed by the army. The SA not only guarded Hitler and his cohorts but also assaulted Hitler's political opponents, communists and Jews, particularly at rallies where Hitler was to speak. The army looked upon the SA as potential recruits for when they could expand the Wehrmacht to more than the 100,000 men that the Versailles treaty permitted.

Among Hitler's long list of policies was ultranationalism, anti-monarchism, a hatred of capitalism, a liking for some socialist ideas (he wanted a classless society), and strong anti-Semitism. He started to attract the attention of wealthy industrialists who saw in him and his party a way of returning Germany to its greatness prior to the First World War, and also a way of stopping left-wing politicians from taxing them. By the end of 1921, The Nazis were the largest right-wing party in Bavaria.[16]

1920 Selve 6/24 specification

Wheelbase:	2,997mm
Engine:	4 cylinders inline, water cooled
Capacity:	1,497cc
Bore × stroke:	72 × 100mm
Valve actuation:	Side valve
Power:	24bhp
Fuel:	Petrol, via one Pallas carburettor
Max speed:	60kph
Gearbox:	4-speed and reverse
Transmission:	Rear-wheel drive

1921 Selve 8/32 specification

Wheelbase:	2,997mm
Engine:	4 cylinders inline, water cooled
Capacity:	2,086cc
Bore × stroke:	85 × 100mm
Valve actuation:	Side valve
Power:	30bhp (Later increased to 32bhp)
Fuel:	Petrol, via one Pallas carburettor
Max speed:	70kph
Gearbox:	4-speed and reverse
Transmission:	Rear-wheel drive
Tyres:	765 × 105

Chapter 2

Growth and Putsch, 1922–24

Hitler was already showing himself to be strongly anti-Semitic by the early 1920s, lumping the Jews in with so-called traitorous financiers and war profiteers who had 'stabbed Germany in the back' in the world war just over. He embarked upon a series of personal speeches across Germany to raise his party's profile and try to bring new members into the fold. In 1920 alone, he made eighty-seven speeches in various venues, most in the Munich area. Hence a car for his own use became ever more important.

This period of the 1920s was a tumultuous time in Germany. Raging inflation gripped a country that was nominally ruled by the government in Weimar but street fighting constantly broke out between the Nazi party and the communists wherever they gathered. Freikorps, many ex-army, acted as a form of right-wing military police and the people of Germany found themselves living in a tormented land.[1]

During 1922, Hitler appointed Heinrich Hoffman, from Munich, as his personal photographer. Previously, Hoffman had attempted to take a photo of Hitler for an American newspaper, which was offering $1,000 for one but when Hoffman attempted to take it, Hitler's bodyguards beat him up and ruined the photo. After this, Hoffman went to see Hitler and showed him a photograph that he had taken in August 1914 that clearly showed Hitler being overwhelmed with joy as the First World War was declared in Munich. Hitler told Hoffman that he would be the only photographer allowed to take photos of him and these would be vetted by him personally, together with Josef Goebbels when he joined the Nazi Party and became the minister for propaganda. Hoffman had been trained in photography, belonging to a reconnaissance squadron of the Luftstreitkräfte in 1917 during the First World War. He had joined the Nazi Party in 1920.[2]

It was at Hoffman's studio that Hitler first met Eva Braun, who later became his mistress. She was working for Hoffman at the time.

At one of the DAP's first meetings, on 4 November 1921, Hitler had risen to make a speech at the Festival Hall of the Hofbräuhaus in Munich. Some 400 communists and Jews had then attempted to break up the meeting and fifty SA (Sturmabteilung) men had fought them. Emil Maurice, later to become a chauffeur of Hitler had been, as usual, in the lead of the SA during the fighting. Five days later, Hitler addressed his SA men thus:

> For us there are only two possibilities: either we remain German or we come under the thumb of the Jews. This latter must not occur; even if we are small, we are a force. A well-organised group can conquer a strong enemy. If you stick close together and keep bringing in new people, we will be victorious over the Jews.[3]

By 1922, Hitler had become the leader of the renamed NSDAP and was now its star speaker. The NSDAP was supported in many ways, particularly financially, by the Thule Society. Apparently, Hitler learned much of the mystique of his speech making, which was, by all accounts mesmerising, from various personages within that society.

What cannot be denied is that the party, whether as the DAP or the NSDAP, always had its hand out looking for political donations, in which it succeeded and this meant that Hitler was introduced to many powerful and rich people, who could afford to give large sums of money to an organisation such as the Nazis, which embodied the conservative principles that such people admired.

Where money was concerned, the average German citizen's situation was dire in the early 1920s, with inflation roaring. Ferry Porsche, the then ten-year-old son of Dr Ferdinand Porsche, who worked in 1922 for Austro-Daimler motor cars, wrote: 'We suffered badly from a postwar currency inflation that left both Austria and Germany almost bankrupt. To give one example, the whole of my father's life insurance policy was not enough to buy a pair of shoes!' He added: 'When I went daily to my private school, I normally took along several million marks with me so that I could buy my ticket for the streetcar ride. After a short time though, I was compelled to walk home because the cost of a streetcar ticket had risen by so many million marks that I no longer could carry enough money.' It was not until after November 1923 that Germany's inflation could be controlled. Of course, Hitler castigated the Weimar Government in his speeches at that time for their inability to control the economy.[4]

Hitler seems to have used the party's bank account as his own during the 1920s and 1930s, and certainly seems to have been on very good terms with the Bavarian tax authorities, who did not charge him all that they should have done at this time.[5]

In 1921, Dietrich Eckart had introduced Hitler to the delights of the countryside around Obersalzberg, near to Berchtesgaden, and after his release from prison in December 1924, Hitler rented a room at the Moritz boarding house and spent many weekends there with his friends and colleagues. He also later on, after 1925, started on a second volume of *Mein Kampf* in Wachenfeld House, which had been the country home of a manufacturer from Buxtehude. This was the property later called the Berghof and Hitler soon moved in there, paying a yearly rent of 1,000 marks. Helene Bechstein, the wife of the head of the piano making company owner, helped with the furnishings and Hitler had his widowed half-sister Angela move in as his housekeeper, together with her daughter, Geli Raubal, who was seventeen at that time. Helene was to prove herself in the future a useful ally of Hitler's, particularly when he needed money ...[6]

It was during these early years of the formation of the Nazi Party that many of the people who would rise to high rank in political power in Germany joined. People such as Rudolf Hess, one of the first members who joined in 1920, became Hitler's secretary and then deputy until his doomed flight to Scotland in May 1941. Hess, like Hitler, had also fought throughout the First World War, been wounded and received the Iron Cross second class. It was Hess who put forward the idea of Lebensraum (living space) to Hitler, to give German people the opportunity to move east into Poland and Russia, when that had been conquered. Hess was close to Hitler and was with him in the failed Putsch in Munich in 1923. While in Landsberg Jail with Hitler, he helped him in the actual writing of *Mein Kampf*.[7]

Herman Goering had been a fighter ace in the First World War, having been promoted to lead the Jagdgeschwader (hunting wing) of Manfred von Richthofen in July 1918, just two months after the famed von Richthofen's death in combat and four months before the Armistice. He had been awarded Germany's highest decoration, the Pour le Mérite, for shooting down twenty-two Allied aircraft. He had first heard Hitler making a speech in November 1922 and was with him in the Munich Putsch in 1923, as commander of the 11,000 strong SA. He was wounded during this, then spirited out of Germany to Austria by his wife to recover. In 1927 he returned to Germany, although he was by then a heroin addict.

Josef Goebbels was one of the few of Hitler's closest friends and colleagues who did not serve in the military in the First World War; he had a club foot and had been rejected on medical grounds for military service. At university he studied literature and history and gained a PhD. He was a rabid anti-Semite and had ambitions to be a writer. Indeed, he had written fourteen books by 1940. He joined the Nazi Party in late 1924 after initially opposing Hitler, and in 1926 became the Gauleiter of Berlin before later being promoted to be Minister of Propaganda.

Heinrich Himmler was the last of this quartet to join the Nazi Party. He was just eighteen in 1918 and had served only with a reserve battalion of the army, never seeing action. He went to university and then joined the Nazi Party in 1923. In 1925 he became a member of the SS. In 1929, Hitler appointed him to the position of Reichsführer-SS and he set about expanding the SS.

Another of Hitler's close circle in Munich in the early 1920s was Dr Ernst F. Sedgwick 'Putzi' Hanfstaengl, a 6ft 6in-tall wealthy graduate of Harvard in 1909. He and his American wife returned to Germany from America in 1922 and in

November, Hanfstaengl went to listen to one of Hitler's speeches and was entranced. Hanfstaengl's father and grandfather had been friends with the Kaiser and his father at their courts. It was Hanfstaengl and his wife who introduced Hitler to the upper classes of Bavarian society, among whom were Helene Bechstein and her husband. Hanfstaengl, writing in 1957, had this to say about them:

> He had been introduced to the Bechstein family, who made their famous pianos in Berlin, but visited Munich frequently. They invited him to dinner at their deluxe hotel in a private suite and he reported on it to me wide-eyed. Frau Bechstein had been 'en grande toilette' and her husband had worn a dinner jacket. 'I felt quite embarrassed in my blue suit,' Hitler told me. 'The servants were all in livery and we drank nothing but champagne before the meal. And you should have seen the bathroom; you can even regulate the heat of the water.'[8]

Early Nazi Party members pose with Hitler in his second car, another Selve, in September 1923. (*Bundesarchiv, Bild 102-00204/CC-BY-SA 3.0*)

In 1923, Hitler visited Dietrich Eckart, who then lived at the Platterhof Hotel in Berchtesgaden and fell in love with the area, later on renting an apartment and then buying the Berghof near there, which became his retreat from Berlin in later years. Hitler used the pseudonym 'Herr Wolf' when he visited Eckart and visited several inns in the area to meet other like-minded people.[9]

John Grehan, in his book, *The Hitler Assassination Attempts, the Plots, Places and People that Almost Changed History* (Frontline, Barnsley, 2022), wrote:

> In April of that year (1923), Hitler and his friend the German-American businessman Ernst 'Putzi' Hanfstaengl were driving in Hitler's green Selve with Nazi Party devotee Emil Maurice at the wheel. At a town on the outskirts of Leipzig, an area largely controlled by Communists, they were stopped at a roadblock manned by 'Red' militia. Hanfstaengl showed the Communists his Swiss passport and in a broad German-American accent told them he had come to visit the Leipzig fair. 'I am a paper manufacturer and printer and I am visiting the Leipzig Fair. This is my valet (pointing to Hitler). My chauffeur and the other gentleman is the son of a German business associate.' The ruse worked and they were allowed to pass through. As they drove away, a relieved Hitler commented that: 'They would have had my head.'[10]

During 1923 also, Hitler enlisted first World War General Erich Ludendorff to help him in trying to attempt a coup in Bavaria. He had seen Mussolini's success on his 'March to Rome' in October 1922, where the Italian had seized power in Italy from the elected government, and determined to try the same tactic in Munich. He had first met Ludendorff in Berlin, in March 1920, when with Dietrich Eckart.

On 8 November, Hitler led several hundred of his followers to surround the beer hall where Gustav von Kahr, the state commissioner of Bavaria, was speaking. Hitler had decided to kidnap him and force him to lead the party to Berlin, where he would overthrow the elected government. Ernst Hanfstaengl wrote: 'It must have been half an hour or more (about 7.30 p.m.) before the red Benz car* he had recently acquired drew up and he climbed out …'

Bursting into the hall, with some twenty supporters, Hitler took out his pistol and fired a shot into the ceiling and then announced that a 'national revolution' was taking place. Von Kahr and two of his colleagues were taken into a separate room, while Ludendorff was informed of what had happened via a telephone call.

---

* Nowhere else can I find any mention of this car of Hitler's, perhaps it belonged to Amann, Rosenberg or Ulrich Graf, who accompanied him. Or perhaps Hanfstaengl is mixing it up with the later Mercedes that Helene Bechstein bought for him in 1925.

Ludendorff arrived shortly thereafter and persuaded the three men to give in to Hitler's demands and march on Berlin.

So far, success had attended Hitler's efforts but when his followers tried to take over government buildings in Munich, they found the military opposing them. The next day, Ludendorff led some 3,000 of Hitler's followers in a March to Munich town centre and found their way blocked by state police. Shooting broke out and four policemen and sixteen Nazi Party members were killed. Despite a dislocated shoulder, Hitler escaped but Ludendorff, scorning the police, walked up to the police. They did not open fire on him. Ludendorff then disassociated himself from Hitler's cause, citing Hitler's cowardice in trying to escape the consequences of his actions.[11]

Hitler went into hiding at the Hanfstaengls' apartment while 'Putzi' Hanfstaengl was away, leaving his wife in charge, but Hitler was discovered and arrested on 11 November. 'Putzi' Hanfstaengl recalled:

> Late on the evening of the Munich putsch a knock came at the door and outside stood Hitler, Dr. Walter Schnitze, a physician in one of the SA battalions, and two or three others. Hitler asked if he could stay the night. My wife, in total ignorance of all that had occurred, let him in and the others went away. She gave him a little attic bedroom I had fitted up with my books, while she slept downstairs with Egon and the maid. Hitler was completely despondent and almost incoherent, but she managed to piece together some sort of account of what had happened.
>
> The next morning my wife told him, 'Herr Hitler, for your own sake you ought to find somewhere else to hide. The police are sure to come here, even if only to look for my husband, and it is too much of a risk.' This he fully understood. The plan was for him to wait for the Bechsteins' car to come and pick him up and take him to safety. So, for the time being, he stayed, spending most of the day in the attic room, where the bed was covered by the two English travelling rugs I had acquired in my student days, which he then took with him to Landsberg prison … on Sunday evening a couple of lorries appeared in the front of the house, full of green-uniformed gendarmery. My wife hurried up to the attic and found Hitler in a state of frenzy. He had pulled out his revolver with his good hand and shouted. 'This is the end. I will never let these swine take me. I will shoot myself first.' It so happened that I had taught my wife one of the few jujitsu tricks I know; how to wrench a pistol out of someone's grasp. Hitler's movements were awkward with his dislocated shoulder and she managed to get the thing away from him and fling it into a two-hundredweight barrel of flour we kept up in the attic to combat the

> recurrent shortages. Hitler calmed down somewhat and in the few moments left sat down and scribbled out a political testament on a piece of paper.
>
> By this time a lieutenant and a couple of gendarmes were at the door. They had just come from my mother's farm, which was nearby, where they had been sticking bayonets in haystacks looking for Hitler, but now felt sure of their quarry. Hitler came downstairs and made no physical resistance, but gave them a terrible tongue-lashing at the top of his voice, accusing them of breaking their oath, conniving at the splitting of Germany and more in the same vein. All this was above the heads of the police, whose loyalties had been veering like weathervanes at the behest of their senior officers over the previous three or four days. So they presented their excuses and politely carried him off.[12]

Hitler and his accomplices, including Ludendorff, were tried for high treason in a trial that lasted for twenty-four days. Hitler used all of his rhetorical skills in the courtroom to create a story about his small, innocent party being the victim, rather than the aggressor. The event catapulted him to national fame and on 26 February 1924 he was sentenced to five years in Landsberg prison, although advised that he would probably only serve six months and then be let out on probation. He was joined there by several others of his followers, including Emil Maurice and Rudolf Hess. The Nazi Party was officially disbanded. Unofficially it was led while 'underground' by Alfred Rosenberg, but he did not do well in the job and Hitler replaced him with Ernst Pöhner, who was little better, by all accounts.[13]

In Landsberg, Hitler was treated leniently, allowed visitors and wrote *Mein Kampf*, by dictating it to Rudolf Hess. This went on to sell in the millions of copies and made Hitler a very rich man. He served less than a year in prison and was released on parole on 20 December 1924.[14]

Where Hitler's cars were concerned, the correspondence below is from 13 September 1924. In this letter to Jakob Werlin, a Mercedes-Benz car salesman in Munich, Hitler, while still in Landsberg, asked for his advice about buying an 11/40 (built between 1923–25 by the Benz factory, and by all accounts not all that successful [author]), or a larger, 16/50 Benz. Translated from the German by Natascha Hoffmeyer:

> Dear Mr. Werlin!
> After reflecting upon our conversation today, I would like to ask you, dear Mr. Werlin, to perhaps intercede for me in two ways. Generally, I am convinced that an 11/40 would suit my present needs. The only thing that is perhaps influencing me is the fact that it runs 300 rotations [revs per minute, author] faster than the 16/50. I would be grateful if you could let me know in your next

letter whether you think a rpm of 2250 isn't so high that a car might suffer in the short run.

As I said, this is the only thing that makes me cautious about the 11/40, because I will not be able to afford a new car in two or three years and I cannot take the time every few years to find better, more lucrative work. However, I would like to ask you to perhaps also inquire into what kind of a rebate I would get with either a 16/50 or an 11/40. Also whether there is an 11/40 available in grey with wire-spoke wheels.

The difficulty for me, of course, is that – even in the case of my release on October 1 – larger revenues from my book will not be available until mid-December, so I am forced to ask for an advance or loan. It goes without saying that several thousand marks make a difference, as I also have to pay my court and legal costs immediately, which are already making my hair stand on end. Thus, I sincerely ask that you put in a good word for me, since my chance of a purchase generally depends on it.

In any event, I would like to ask you to reserve the grey car you have in Munich until I have clarity regarding my fate (probation?). I will let you know immediately whether I will be released in October and whether I will be able to buy a car.

Yours most respectfully,
Adolf Hitler[15]

Jakob Werlin, far left, explaining a technicality to Hitler at the Berlin Motor Show. Hermann Goering, head of the Luftwaffe, stands to the right of Hitler.

Reading this letter, and observing that Hitler did not get out of prison in October, he probably had this first Benz, the 11/40 described in the letter, demonstrated to him in December 1924, when he was picked up from Landsberg. He may have tried this Benz from Jakob Werlin on that December day in 1924. According to several sources, it was Werlin who picked him up from Landsberg Prison on 20 December 1924 in the grey Benz 11/40, with wire wheels (although Wulf Schwarzwaller, in his book *The Unknown Hitler*, wrote that it was Adolf Mueller, the printer of the *Völkischer Beobachter*, who picked Hitler up in a Mercedes, together with Heinrich Hoffman) and drove him back to his accommodation. We can, however, identify the car that Hitler is standing by in the photo that Hoffman took of him that day as a Benz 11/40. Hitler would not deviate from owning this marque, particularly when it became Mercedes-Benz in 1926, for the rest of his life.[16]

That Benz 11/40 was grey, as opposed to the lighter green colour of Hitler's previous Selve, and had valves mounted in an L-disposition in the six-cylinder engine of 2,860cc (72 × 117mm bore and stroke), fitted with a Zenith twin carburettor, which produced some 40bhp at 2,250rpm. The drive went via a cone clutch to a four-speed gearbox and thence via a prop shaft to the rear wheels. Suspension was conventional for the time, leaf springs suspending beam axles. Either wire or wooden spoke wheels could be ordered (but we can see that the car that Mueller/Werlin came in had wire wheels) and the maximum speed was a heady 50mph. The quoted price was 18,000 Reichsmarks.[17]

Hitler later wrote about his release: 'I left all my money, 234 marks, with my comrades in Landsberg. I returned to Munich in abject poverty.' That was not quite accurate … Helene Bechstein had deposited 45,000 marks in the Hansa bank for him.[18]

Hoffman took Hitler's photo of him standing next to the grey Benz car, labelled as 'Adolf Hitler upon release from Landsberg Prison'. Incidentally, the prison authorities would not let Hoffman photograph Hitler and the Benz outside the prison gates, so Hoffman had to find another location that resembled the prison entrance. He found such a location at one of the old entrances to the city itself.[19]

Jakob Werlin worked for the Benz motor company from 1921, in Munich, Bavaria. He met and grew friendly with Hitler in 1923. The Benz dealership where Werlin worked as a salesman was next door where the Nazi Party newspaper, the *Völkischer Beobachter* (People's Observer), was printed. This was the newspaper created first of all by the Thule Society in 1918. It had first been named the *Münchener Beobachter* (Munich Observer) but with a need to improve its circulation, it was renamed the *Münchener Beobachter und Sportblatt* (Munich Observer and Sports Paper). Now it became a newspaper by and for the Nazi Party. It had originally started as a weekly newspaper, and the first edition was published on 25 December 1920. In

Adolf Hitler leaving Landsberg Prison on 20 December 1924. He was detained there for a total of 264 days for his part in the Beer Hall Putsch in Munich. He is seen here beside the Benz 11/40 that he was picked up in.

December, suffering financial difficulties, it was resold to the Nazi Party, Dietrich Eckart and Ernst Röhm being able to persuade Röhm's old commanding officer, Major General Franz Ritter von Epp, to use money from Wehrmacht funds for this. Eckart mortgaged his house and possessions to secure this deal. By 1921, Adolf Hitler had acquired all the shares of the new company. From 8 February 1923, it became a daily newspaper. In November 1923, after the Munich Putsch, it was banned but resumed publication in 26 February 1925, when the Nazi Party was relaunched. At its height in the 1930s/40s, the paper was selling up to 1.7 million copies daily.[20]

Emil Maurice, following Ernst Haug, was Hitler's next chauffeur, from early 1925 after Hitler had left Landsberg, and he was an early member of the Nazi Party (Number 594 of the preceding DAP). Maurice was an early foot soldier in the SA, and although being of Jewish descent, was declared an 'Honorary Aryan' by Hitler for being at the forefront of the SA in their many brawls with Jews and communists, particularly in the early days of Hitler's rise to power.

1925 Benz 11/40 specification

Wheelbase:	3,274mm
Front Track:	1,350mm
Rear Track:	1,350mm
Length:	4,600mm
Width:	1,740mm
Height:	1,950mm
Weight:	1,600kg
Engine:	6 cylinders inline, water cooled
Capacity:	2,860cc
Bore × stroke:	72 × 117mm
Valve actuation:	Side valve
Power:	40bhp at 2,250rpm
Fuel:	Petrol, via one Zenith carburettor
Fuel tank:	65 litres
Gearbox:	4-speed and reverse
Clutch:	Leather cone
Transmission:	Rear-wheel drive
Maximum speed:	80kph
Tyres:	765 × 105

Chapter 3

The First Mercedes, 1925–1931

On 23 March 1925, Helene Bechstein, one of Hitler's wealthy friends, bought Hitler a Daimler-built Mercedes 15/70/100, which was later renamed the Mercedes-Benz Typ 400 after the two companies, Daimler and Benz, merged in mid-1926. Reputedly, the new car's cost was 26,000 Reichsmarks but this probably included taxes.[1]

The Bechsteins, husband and wife, had been friends with Hitler for some years. In fact at one point, as we have seen, they had been going to spirit Hitler away from his friends, the Hanfstangls, to whose apartment he had fled after the abortive Munich Putsch but the police had arrived there first.[2]

This 1925 Mercedes 15/70/100 was in place of the '11/40' that Hitler had referred to in his letter to Jakob Werlin. The price of the Benz 11/40 was quoted as being 18,000 Reichsmarks. This is far below the 25,000–26,000 Reichsmarks that Mrs Bechstein is reputed to have spent on Hitler's first Mercedes, so we must presume that this car referred to was actually the 15/70/100 model instead, a much better car (more power, more space), which would have enabled Hitler to travel more easily from one speech-making venue to the next.

What we do know is that from February 1925, when Helene Bechstein ordered/paid for the new Mercedes for Hitler (and which was delivered on 23 March), only this Mercedes 4-litre 15/70/100 and its bigger brother, the 6.3-litre 24/100/140, were now available as Mercedes-Benz passenger cars to be bought from Daimler-Benz by the public, the two other Benz models that Hitler had inquired about with Jakob Werlin having been discontinued from their catalogue.[3]

Whether or not Helene Bechstein paid for Hitler's new Mercedes, it came from Jakob Werlin's dealership in Munich and was reported by Wulf Schwarzwaller as: 'A Mercedes Compressor car at the steep price of 20,000 marks.' This, of course, was the 15/70/100 Mercedes that Hitler used for more than six years of his tumultuous climb to the top. It is probable that Hitler traded in the old Selve that he already had in the deal and that perhaps explains the discrepancy between 20,000 and 25,000 Reichsmarks in the price. Schwarzwaller also reported: 'When the finance office asked Hitler where he'd got the money for such an expensive purchase, he said he'd taken out a bank loan.'[4]

Later on, during one of his monologues at the Führer headquarters, Hitler recounted that (as reported by Heinrich Heims, one of Martin Bormann's aides, in 1942):

> The first thing I did on leaving the prison at Landsberg on 20 December 1924 was to buy my supercharged Mercedes. Although I've never driven it myself, I've always been passionately keen on cars.
>
> Adolf Mueller had taught me to drive alright, but I knew that at the slightest accident, my conditional liberty would be withdrawn, and I also knew that nothing would have been more agreeable to the government.
>
> In 1925, my Mercedes Compressor was a joy for everyone. We went on trips to Luisenburg and then again to Bamberg and would often go to Eremiage. Mrs Bechstein had said: 'Wolf [Hitler's name for himself], you simply must have the most beautiful car there is. You deserve it.' She had been thinking of a Maybach.[5]

At one point, Hitler even claimed credit for designing the fabulous late 1930s model Mercedes 500 and 540K roadsters, saying at the same time: 'I can claim credit for

Upon its release, the new Mercedes 15/70/100 was heavily promoted by the factory in 1925.

the things that make Mercedes cars so beautiful today. In drawings and designs, I tried hard year after year to perfect that shape to the utmost.' Certainly, Hitler sketched out a design for the first humble Volkswagen Beetle that was remarkably like the car that emerged from the plant at the Wolfsburg factory.[6]

After his release from prison Hitler was able to return to his previous task of making the Nazi Party the most successful in Germany, although it had been banned in many, but not all, states. Mainly by giving many speeches around the country, Hitler threw himself into the task with renewed energy, promising a better life for Germans, with territories taken away from Germany reclaimed and the guilty politicians of the Weimar Republic punished. Now, he and his chauffeur were covering many kilometres of German roads so that Hitler could make speeches anywhere and everywhere that he could draw a crowd. This is why he needed a car of quality and reliability. Hence the new Mercedes-Benz.

Something else that Hitler did in his various Mercedes cars that followed the 15/70/100 was to attend parades. Hitler and the Nazi Party well understood the importance of showing himself and his forces, first of all the SA and later the SS, and the armed forces wherever and whenever possible. He used the anniversaries of various German holidays, his birthday, 20 April, and, of course, his attendance at the great Nazi saluting base in Nuremberg every September, after that was built in the early 1930s. On these occasions, Hitler's car would lead a phalanx of other vehicles filled with various Nazi dignitaries through the streets at a slow pace, with him standing up and acknowledging the crowds. Flowers would sometimes be strewn on the street ahead of him. It was a new way of showing himself and the spectacle of the Nazi Party to the people.

On 26 February 1925 the *Völkischer Beobachter* published an editorial entitled 'A New Beginning', written by Hitler. Before this was published, Hitler had promised the Prime Minister of Bavaria he would behave himself if his ban on his speaking in public was lifted. The Prime Minister acquiesced, as Hitler now promised to work within the rules of the democratic constitution.

A day later, the Nazis were reunited for the first time since the Beer Hall Putsch. Hitler resumed his position as leader of the party and then gave a speech, during which he overreached himself and started spouting the same old threats against democracy in Germany, the Jews and the communists. He was promptly banned from public speaking for two years by the authorities. This gave Hitler the time and opportunity to completely reorganise his party.

In his reorganisation, Hitler formed PO 1 and PO 2. PO 1 was aimed at demoralising and then overthrowing the democratic republic, while PO 2 was formed as a mirror of the German government. It was a 'shadow' government with Departments of the Interior, Justice, Agriculture, Propaganda, Race and Culture, the Economy and Foreign Affairs, all ready to take over when Hitler became Chancellor.

The Nazi Party divided 'their' Germany up into thirty-four districts, or Gaue, each having a Gauleiter at its head. There were also districts known as Kreise, with a Kreisleiter leading each of these. Within the Kreise were Ortsgruppen, small, local groups.

The Hitler Jugend (Hitler Youth) was formed for boys aged between fourteen and eighteen. It closely mimicked the Boy Scout movement and in the years to come there would be many fights between the boys in these organisations. For girls, there was the Bund Deutsche Mädel. Frauenschaften was a group formed for older women.[7]

Ironically, having been relatively successful in Bavaria, and some other parts of Germany, the Nazi Party now, in the late 1920s, began to find their appeal diminishing. This was because America was investing in Germany.

Charles G. Dawes was an American banker, who had suggested reducing Germany's war reparations by granting loans to that country. He had drawn up a plan, approved by the Allies, that reduced these payments and loaned money to businesses and industry. Now the Reichsmark stabilised, instead of falling against other currencies. German industry started to recover as the government borrowed large sums of money from the USA to help to build its municipal programme.[8]

Apart from the army's financing of the SA, the German armed forces, the Heer, also secretly engaged with Russia to host new training grounds, including for the fledgling new Luftwaffe, and gliding schools for young men sprang up all over Germany, and in Russia too.

Hitler would have to wait until the Wall Street crash of 1929 impoverished many Germans, and turned them into converts for his movement. This may be the reason that the party did not buy Hitler a new car when his Mercedes 15/70/100 was three years old in 1928. They may not have seen it as a worthwhile expenditure at the time. Nevertheless, Hitler never stopped planning for the day that he would take power and endlessly dreamt up ways of helping German industry.

By all accounts, Hitler was very interested in all engineering matters and could converse with qualified engineers at a relatively high level. He always took a keen interest in the cars that he rode in, the aircraft of the Luftwaffe and the armoured vehicles of the Luftwaffe. In fact, it was due to this technical interest that Hitler stopped the groundbreaking gas turbine-powered Messerschmitt Me 262 from going into production in 1942–43 as a fighter. He insisted that it was built as a 'Blitz' (Lightning) bomber and thus put back its introduction into front-line service by a year, which was at a critical juncture of Germany's position, especially in the war in the air at that time. With hindsight, one can see that as a jet fighter over

Germany, the Me 262 may have had a crippling effect on the bombing campaign then just being started by the American Air Force by day.[9]

After Helene Bechstein bought the Mercedes 15/70/100 from Jakob Werlin for Hitler's use in 1925, Hitler would order all his new Mercedes-Benz cars from him in Munich, with the factory's assistance, particularly once Hitler came to power in 1933.

In 1926, when Daimler merged with Benz to form Mercedes-Benz, Werlin started his own Mercedes dealership in Munich, Niederlassung München, and in 1934, he joined Hitler's Nazi Party. Werlin survived the war and, after a spell in an American internment camp, was released in 1948. He then went back to Munich and started his Mercedes-Benz dealership again, now called the Vertriebsgemeinschaft Werlin at Hochstrasse 14. The Mercedes company granted Werlin this dealership, as he had protected Bimbo Haspel during the war. She had been the Jewish wife of Wilhelm Haspel, the chairman of Daimler-Benz from 1942 to 1952.[10]

From 1925, Hitler could be seen in his Mercedes 15/70/100 attending Nazi Party rallies and being driven to give speeches. By now a convert to Mercedes-Benz, Hitler was particularly impressed by the quality of its workmanship and later on credited the manufacturer with him surviving a pair of accidents and emerging virtually unharmed from them.[11]

In 1925, Hitler ordered the formation, with Hauptmann Ernst Röhm's SA to begin with, of the Schutzstaffel (the SS, in English: 'Protection Squadron'). The first staffel so formed was called the Leibstandarte, or 'Bodyguard'. It went on to become one of the most feared divisions of the Waffen SS, the military component of the SS. Dressed in menacing black uniforms, they were led on their formation by Joseph Berchtold. One of its first members was a certain Heinrich Himmler.[12]

Hitler was SS member number 1 and Emil Maurice, who became Hitler's chauffeur in 1925, was number 2. Maurice was later dismissed from Hitler's service in 1928 after admitting having an affair with Hitler's half-niece, Geli Raubal, although he remained a member of the SS. His duties as Hitler's chauffeur were taken over by Julius Schreck.

Schreck had, like Hitler, served in the army in the First World War. In 1920, he joined the Nazi Party and became friendly with Hitler. It was Schreck who decided that the skull and crossbones insignia should be that of the newly formed SS, which was created expressly as Hitler's bodyguard. Schreck became its first commander.[13]

Thuringia was one of the few states in Germany where Hitler was not banned from speaking at this time and in 1926 the Nazi Party held a rally there, at Weimar. Some 5,000 members of Hitler's SA marched past him, giving him the fascist salute of the outstretched right arm, as Roman soldiers had done to their emperor in times gone by. Heinrich Hoffman took many photos at this rally and they were used in the *Völkischer Beobachter*, which sold thousands of copies of that issue alone.[14]

During the 1920s and '30s there was no television. In Germany, there was only the radio and newspapers to keep people informed. Therefore, it was comparatively easy to let the population know only what their political masters wanted them to know. Hence the importance of the *Völkischer Beobachter* to the Nazis.

Always having to have the latest and greatest, in order to impress both his followers and those who might be tempted to join the party, Hitler, by 1925, very much liked his new Mercedes-Benz 15/70/100. In this nomenclature, the Ferdinand Porsche-designed car* had an inline six-cylinder, overhead camshaft engine of 3,921cc capacity, with a 'Kompressor' (supercharger), added. The power was fed via a multi-plate dry clutch through a four-speed gearbox to the rear axle, via an enclosed torque tube. In early cars the gear lever was mounted, as was the practice in the early to mid-1920s, outside the bodywork but it was later repositioned to a central position, between the driver's and the passenger's seats. Suspension was by beam axles front and rear, suspended on semi-elliptical springs, diagonal stabilising rods fitted beneath the torque tube, and connecting to the wheel hubs, and the four-wheel brakes were cable operated.

The supercharger compressed the incoming air to the engine, thus increasing its power, and Mercedes had been using this for several years on their racing sportscars, the 'S', 'SS', 'SSK' and 'SSKL' models, which, respectively, stood for 'Sport', 'Super Sport', 'Super Sport Kurz' (Kurz = Short, the chassis was shortened), and 'Super Sport Short Light'. They were to carry on in production until after 1930.

The Roots-type supercharger blew the compressed air through the updraught carburettor, allowing the fuel to mix with the air before passing through the inlet manifold, into the combustion chambers. The supercharger emitted an impressive piercing scream when the accelerator was pushed to the floor. So '15' stood for taxable horsepower (a measurement based on bore and stroke of the engine to give its taxable value), '70' stood for naturally aspirated (non-supercharged) horsepower (or 'PS' in German terms) and '100' stood for the horsepower developed when the supercharger was employed at peak rpm.

From 1925, the Typ 400 15/70/100 could be had with four- or six-seater open-bodied Tourenwagen bodywork; a six-seater Landaulet; a six-seater Pullman-Limousine; a four-door, four-seater Cabriolet; or a six-seater Coupe-Limousine, all by the Mercedes bodywork factory in Sindelfingen. For customers who wanted

* Ferdinand Porsche had succeeded Paul Daimler as the chief designer at Mercedes-Benz on 30 April 1923.

something different, they could purchase a rolling chassis and have it bodied by one of the many bodybuilders in existence at the time.

During its production run, from February 1925 to February 1929, Mercedes-Benz sold 1,943 15/70/100 cars and they were succeeded by the Typ W08 Nürburg 460/500 and then the W07 'Grosser' Mercedes-Benz in 1930.

The Mercedes-Benz 15/70/100 Tourenwagen had a length of over 16ft and was almost 6ft wide. The car was developed using the knowledge that had been gained by Mercedes-Benz with their racing sports cars. This resulted in an imposingly large, expensive car, which for its day was fast, at 70mph maximum speed. Unlike many Mercedes-Benz 15/70/100s, Hitler's car had left-hand drive, at a time when most cars of this type were right-hand drive. This allowed Hitler, standing in the front passenger compartment, to be nearer to the crowd on his side.[15]

The Mercedes press release for both the 15/70/10 and its bigger brother, the 24/100/140, said:

> Thanks to their inherent smoothness and flexibility, combined with fast acceleration and high reserves of power, the two vehicles make an ideal tourer

The engine of a 1930 Mercedes-Benz SS 'Kompressor' of 1930. This was a development of the engine used in the 15/70/100. The supercharger is at the left, at the front of the engine. (*Photo courtesy of author*)

cum sports car, an outstanding hill-climber and – as gear-changing is required only on exceptionally steep uphill slopes – a most convenient town car for the expert motorist.

From its lowest through to its highest revolutions, the completely silent, carefully balanced engine guarantees an effortless transition and high torque even at low engine speeds.

About the bodywork, Mercedes press department said:

> Also the coachwork of the new models represents a significant advance.
>
> Thanks to the amply available length and width, both models allow seven-seater bodies with deep seats and four large doors. The low frame height ensures effortless entry and exit.

An official poster by Daimler-Benz, showing off their two new models, the 15/70/100 and the 24/100/140.

> The Mercedes coachwork is the supreme expression of comfort and elegance. It was designed in perfect taste by top artists and manufactured in unsurpassed excellence of workmanship at the coachworks in Sindelfingen.

The Typ 400, along with the Typ 630 (6.3 litres, 24/100/140 designation), went on display for the first time at the Berlin Motor Show, held in December 1924. Normally the show was held in September but due to the poor state of the economy at the time, the show was postponed for two months. The stated price for the Typ 400 was RM 22,750 and for the Typ 630, RM 27,750.

One of the few other cars to compete for sales with the Mercedes Typ 400 at the time was the British-built Bentley 3-litre, a four-cylinder car with, like the Mercedes, an overhead camshaft engine. That was succeeded in 1927 by the 4.5-litre Bentley, that having a six-cylinder engine, also with an overhead camshaft, like the Typ 400 and Typ 630. Incidentally, W.O. Bentley himself had attended the Rolls-Royce factory in August 1914, when the mechanics/fitters of that company had stripped down the French Grand Prix-winning Mercedes race car, and 'took copious notes' about its construction. Bentley undoubtedly used that knowledge when he designed his first automobile engines in the early 1920s.[16]

In 1925, that other maker of cars for the top end of the market in England was Rolls-Royce. They were in 1925 just starting to produce their new Phantom model, which replaced the Silver Ghost. This was also known as the 40/50. The size of this six-cylinder, overhead valve engine was 7,668cc and it drove the rear wheels through a four-speed and reverse gearbox and an enclosed torque tube to the rear axle. The chassis was a carry-over from the previous Silver Ghost, with semi-elliptical springs supporting beam axles, and in the cars built in England, four-wheel drum brakes were used, together with a licensed Hispano-Suiza servo. Some of the cars built at Rolls-Royce USA, in Springfield, Massachusetts, had only two wheel brakes and a three-speed and reverse gearbox. A total of 3,509 cars were built between 1925 and 1931.

The registration of Hitler's first supercharged Mercedes was IIA-6629, a Munich plate, and he was photographed in it on many occasions, usually with his old comrade, Julius Schreck chauffeuring him to his various appointments. One of the big advantages over its rivals, where Hitler's use was concerned, was that with four large doors, and a low chassis height, entrance and exit were easy. Not something that could be said for every passenger car of that period.

It would appear from photos that Hitler used this Typ 400 as his own car from 1925, when it was bought for him, until 1931, when the new W07 Grosser

Mercedes-Benz was introduced. This seems an unusually long time but certainly there is an invoice available showing that a 15/70/100, belonging to Hitler (the invoice shows his private address) had a front spring replaced in October 1928 by the dealer. The engine number is shown as being '48045', so presumably the car's chassis number was W (for Wagen) 48045.

As a mark of Hitler's rising prestige, wealth and popularity among the party and voters, Hitler moved, in October 1929, into a nine-room apartment at 16, Prinz Regent Square, opposite the Prince Regent Theatre, so now he could walk over the street to see his favourite operas by Wagner. The rent of his new apartment was 4,176 marks annually. Hitler still referred to himself as a 'painter and author'. Fritz Thyssen, the son of Germany's richest man, August Thyssen, who had founded the United Steel Works, was now, after his father's death, the sole heir to his fortune in 1926. Two years later, Thyssen arranged a loan of well over a million marks, so that

Hitler returning the salute of a parade of SA stormtroopers in Weimar on 12 October 1930. Note his then deputy, Rudolf Hess behind him. Hitler is in his first Mercedes-Benz, the 15/70/100 still. (*Bundesarchiv; Bild 102-10541*)

the Nazi Party could buy their new headquarters, the Barlow Palace on Brienner Strasse in Munich, later known as the Brown House.

Sometime shortly prior to this move, Hitler told Thyssen of his own financially 'precarious position'. Thyssen immediately arranged to pay all of Hitler's bank debts and to fund his move into a more upmarket home. He would pay all his expenses, including those of Hitler's personal staff.[17]

Although he used his 15/70/100 for a long time, Hitler was pictured several times in a Typ W08 Nürburg 460 in 1930, and in October 1934 in another Nürburg, this time a 500, both with the same Munich registration, II-22006. Was the registration moved over as the original car was damaged in Hitler's crash of 1931? Or perhaps the first car was traded in? Although it was a Mercedes-Benz, it is difficult to find details of that car.[18]

Hitler kept his now old Mercedes 15/70/100 well into 1931. He had probably grown quite fond of it. After all, it was his first Mercedes. Although we don't know for sure, it's probable that he traded it in in 1931 in a part-exchange deal with Jakob Werlin's Mercedes-Benz dealership back in Munich for his first W07 Grosser.

1924–26: Mercedes 15/70/100 PS

Manufacturer:

1924–26:	Daimler-Benz Gesellschaft
1926–29:	Daimler-Benz AG

Type:

1925–29:	Mercedes-Benz 15/70/100 PS
1927–29:	Mercedes-Benz Typ 400

Built in Stuttgart, Germany.

Body and chassis: Either an Offener Tourenwagen (open tourer), a Limousine (enclosed sedan), or a Landaulet (four-door cabriolet). The car could also be purchased as a rolling chassis and a body built/bought separately.

Engine

Bore × stroke:	80mm × 130mm
Six cylinders inline:	3,920cc, supercharged. (Kompressor)
Valve actuation:	SOHC, via rockers
Compression ratio:	4.7:1
Max. Power:	100bhp @ 3,100rpm

Dimensions

Wheelbase:	3,630mm (143in)
Length:	4,960mm (195in)
Width:	1,780mm (70in)
Height:	1,950mm (77in)

Chapter 4

Mercedes-Benz W07 Grosser 770, 1930–37

In 1930, Mercedes-Benz introduced their new, top-of-the-line prestigious car, very refined, and very expensive at that time, ranging from 38,000 Reichsmarks for a Pullman Limousine without a supercharger, up to 47,500 Reichsmarks for a Cabriolet with all the available options.

The new 'Grosser' (Great, Grand, Super) Mercedes-Benz W07 was indeed a lavish car, meant for the very rich, and the nobility.

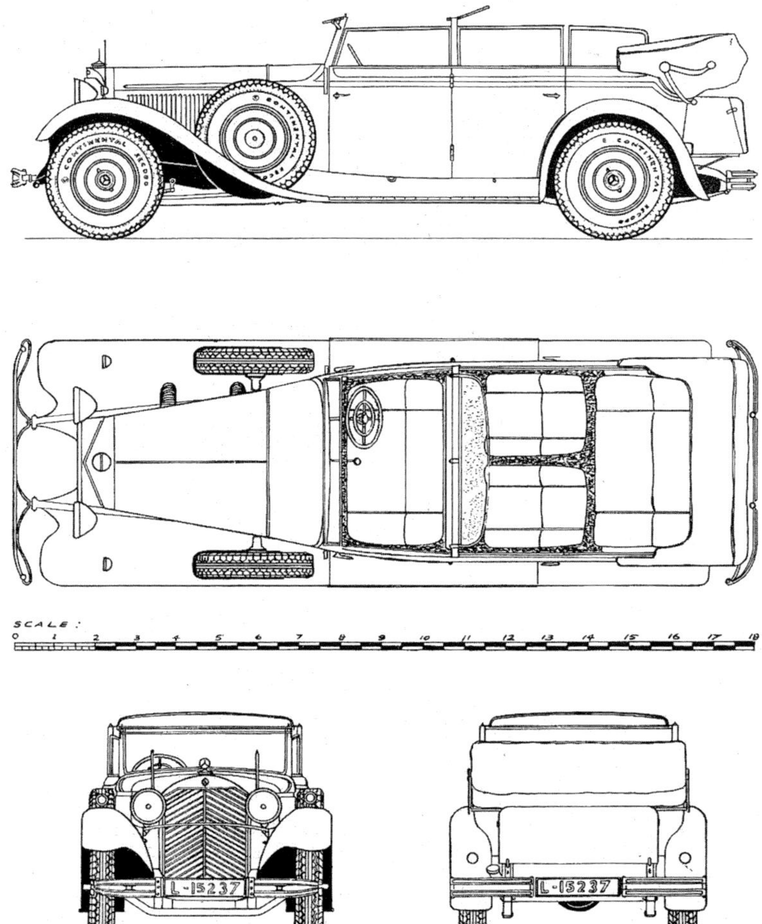

Four views on the 1930 Mercedes-Benz Typ W07 Grosser 770. This car is today in the Mercedes-Benz Museum.

It was only one year since the Wall Street crash and most of the world, including Germany, was in the middle of a financial crisis.[1] Paradoxically, this new financial disaster was to lead to the success of Hitler and the Nazi Party; for many, particularly in the countryside, now saw Hitler and his party as the only people who could set Germany onto a better path, particularly economically. Indeed, once Hitler came to power and set about reducing unemployment, particularly by building autobahns and promoting the manufacture of armaments, Germany's prosperity took on a new tone, improving year upon year.

Hitler's own finances improved in 1930. *Mein Kampf* sold 54,000 copies and he had negotiated a 15 per cent commission of the sale price for himself. His cut of the sales amounted to 46,000 Marks. Sales increased steadily in the 1930s: 50,808 in 1931, 90,351 in 1932, for which Hitler received 65,000 Marks and, in 1933, the book sold 854,127 copies. Hitler was now a rich man, although publicly he insisted that he was still poor, just working as the head of the Nazi Party for the good of the people.[2]

Hitler personally inspected the open-air preserve called the Luitpoldhain on 13 March 1930, which he intended to convert into a rallying area for the party faithful. This was located to the south-east of Nuremberg and the project was duly carried out. While returning to base, the Mercedes-Benz 15/70/100 that Hitler was riding in (driving?) collided with a Magirus truck.

Otto Wagener was in the backseat. He remembered:

> In silence, we got back in the car for the return drive …
>
> As we were about to cross the wide avenue in the south-east of the city that led to the centre from the stadium – on a crossing that widened into a small, triangular open space – from the right, a monster of a truck, hauling an equally overpowering trailer, came rushing ahead at a fairly rapid rate, only ten or fifteen metres from us.
>
> We ourselves had slowed down to a speed of about 20kph. Our driver at first stepped onto the accelerator and if only he had driven on, nothing at all would have happened. But – the devil knows why! – he braked abruptly in an effort to let the truck pass.
>
> Its driver however – we subsequently learned that he did not even have a licence, while the man who was the nominal operator sat next to him – though he braked as well, at the same time stepped on the gas, and while the real driver grabbed the wheel to rectify the situation, turned left, that is straight at us, assuming that we would simply drive on. And so, this monster of a vehicle came rushing at our almost immobile car!
>
> I can still see the large letters 'Magirus' over me as the powerful radiator pushed its way over our car's body, pressing Hitler, Hess, and myself to the

> left of the car. Then the truck's frame and springs must have taken hold of our Mercedes and shoved it diagonally across the open triangle, a distance of about twenty metres, as far as the street corner, only to come to a stop at last at the instant when our left wheels were already touching the curb.'
>
> Only a short stretch more, and the left wheels would have broken, and the monster would've run over and crushed the passengers. After a few moments, the truck – with a terrible grinding of the motor, which was on top of us, reversed for a few metres and pulled its projecting radiator off us. Hitler was the first to regain his voice. 'Everyone still alive?' When I called out my assurance, he said: 'In fact nothing could have happened to us! We have not yet completed our task!'[3]

Hitler remembered that: 'The other car (truck?) was totally wrecked. On mine only the bumpers and running board were damaged. It was then I decided to use only a Mercedes for the rest of my life.'

Hitler, still in his 1925 Mercedes 15/70/100 in April 1931. (*Polish National Archives*)

Adolf Hitler in a Mercedes Typ W07 Grosser 770 car in Berlin in August 1932. Next to him visible, among others, are Wilhelm Frick, and Hitler's official photographer, Heinrich Hoffmann.

There is an insurance document extant, concerning this accident, dated 17 October 1930, with Hitler's name on it and stating that it involved his 1925 Mercedes 15/70/100, but it may be that that was because the car was in his name, not that he was the driver. According to the document, Hitler's motor insurance company settled his claim for damage caused on 13 March 1930 to his Mercedes. The owner of the document recorded: 'The document is the acknowledgement returned by Adolf Hitler after he received money from the insurance company for the repair of his car after an auto accident in 1930. The document mentions the accident and repair to his 1925 Mercedes saloon.'

The German government called an election for 14 September 1930, and on that day, after a whirlwind campaign, most of it organised by Joseph Goebbels, the Nazi Party finished up with 6,371,000 votes (the German population at the time was some 60 million). This gave the party 107 seats in the government, the Reichstag. From nowhere (a mere 100,000 party members), the Nazis had moved to second place among the political parties in Germany.

Suddenly Hitler, well known in Germany, became internationally famous. Foreign newspaper editors wanted stories about him. When the time came for them to be seated in the Reichstag on 13 October 1930, the elected Nazi deputies, dressed in brown shirts, marched in. As each one was sworn in, he shouted, 'Present! Heil Hitler!'[4]

It was during this momentous time that Hitler urged on the motorisation of the Reich, promoting Adolf Hühnlein to oversee motoring developments via the Motor Korps (NSKK) in 1930.

Hühnlein was born at Neustädtlein bei Kulmbach on 12 September 1881, and after service in the First World War, by 1918 he was serving in the anti-Bolshevik Freikorps, which put down the communist revolt in Munich in 1919.

In 1923 Hühnlein was a staff officer in the early SA and he took part in the attempted Beer Hall Putsch in Munich of 8–9 November. He became the Quartermaster for its membership in 1925 and was obviously a good organiser.

Martin Bormann, who was in 1929 assistant to Hitler's private secretary Rudolf Hess, discussed with Hitler that the SA motor squadrons were lacking direction. He wrote that: 'The Party would greatly benefit from having a nationwide pool of motorised transport to enable rapid mobilisation during a show of strength.'

Hühnlein became the head of the SA's Motor Corps, founding at the same time the Automobile Corps (NSAK), the SA Motor Troops, and later on the Motor Korps (NSKK).

In 1932, Hühnlein became a lieutenant general and after Hitler became Reich Chancellor on 30 January 1933 he oversaw the complete German motor establishment, encouraging automobile production, ownership and racing. Hühnlein was carrying out Der Führer's wishes of a complete motorisation of Germany.

In 1934, the NSKK became an independent organisation and now Hühnlein was responsible to Hitler only. NSKK members took part in the annual congresses at Nuremberg for the first time by helping with transportation. There were now 350,000 members of the NSKK.[5]

It was during this time that Hitler decided to encourage German manufacturers to build and enter race cars in what was then called grand prix racing, which morphed into what is today's F1. To this end, he – or rather the German taxpayer – subsidised both Mercedes-Benz and the Ferdinand Porsche-designed Auto Union establishment, based at Zwickau. The cars that resulted from this initiative dominated international motor racing at the top level before the war, crushing all before them. Famous names in racing such as Bugatti, Alfa Romeo and Maserati

2

Freepost Plus RTKE-RGRJ-KTTX
Pen & Sword Books Ltd
47 Church Street
BARNSLEY
S70 2AS

could not compete with this onslaught. Hühnlein was the political head of this project.

All German males were compelled to join the NSKK when they were aged 20½ to 21 before going into the Wehrmacht, the Luftwaffe or the Kreigsmarine. These trained men became messengers and motorcycle scouts, and the drivers of tanks, staff cars and trucks during the war. There were more than 3.2 million cars and trucks on German roads in 1937, and in 1938, the membership of the NSKK had risen to 500,000 men.

By 1939, over 200,000 young German men had been trained to drive. The NSKK regulated traffic on German roads, acting as a motorist's roadside help in the case of accidents and breakdowns. Hitler believed that drivers and not pedestrians were responsible for accidents between cars and pedestrians, and fines and penalties for speeding and fatalities caused by drivers were harsh.

It may be thought that Hitler and his Nazi Party were completely in the ascendant in German politics at this time but by 1931 they were facing a strong government coalition of the centre left, dominated by the Social Democratic Party. They were often backed by the Reichsbanner, a veterans' association that counted, ironically, among its members Karl Mayr, Hitler's commander in intelligence matters in 1919. The Reichsbanner spoke in support of preventing future wars by way of international co-operation and collective security. In 1931, for instance, Mayr gave a speech on 22 February at a gathering at one of Munich's biggest beer halls, where over 2,000 people had gathered to hear him and others speak.[6]

To replace the open touring Mercedes 15/70/100 of the type that Hitler had been using until 1931, the new company had produced the Mercedes-Benz Typ Nürburg 460 and later on the 500 (W08), which sold surprisingly well, considering the financial privations taking place worldwide at this time. There were several years of strong growth in German car sales during these years but this was probably caused by the galvanising effect that Hitler and his party had on the country upon taking control in 1933.[7]

Before that, as recounted by Ferry, son of Ferdinand Porsche:

> To get a close-up idea of how rapidly things could change almost on your doorstep, there was the case of Jakob Werlin, a director of Daimler-Benz whose contract had been cancelled because he happened to be a friend of Adolf Hitler while his rise to power was still in question. Werlin, who had been on excellent terms with my father for a long time, simply came to him and complained, 'I'm now without a job.' As it turns out, when Hitler came into power, Werlin was given a new contract by Daimler-Benz with an even better job than before.[8]

Development of the new W07 car by Mercedes-Benz had started in 1928. At that time, Daimler-Benz was producing and selling their six-cylinder Typ 400, or 15/70/100 (of which Hitler had one, registered as II-6629, from 1925), and the 630 and 630K six-cylinder cars for those who could afford them. In September 1930, a memo to the dealers announced that the new 'Grosser Mercedes' would put all of Mercedes-Benz's previous models in the shade when it debuted in October 1930 at the Motor and Cycle show held at the Grand Palais in Paris. The unsupercharged, eight-cylinder Typ W08 Nürburg had, as we have seen, been introduced in 1928 but the Mercedes-Benz directors realised that something much better was needed to match their competitors in their hunt for rich, prestigious customers.

Customers attending the International Paris motor show in October 1930 saw the new W07 make its debut. November was the date that customers could expect to receive the first Grosser cars, notably in Pullman Limousine form from the body plant at Sindelfingen. Open bodywork would be provided by Joseph Neuss, Erdman and Rossi and Voll and Ruhrbeck. Customers wanting special features in their bodywork could have them executed by the Sonderwagenbau, a department at the Sindelfingen factory that catered to these tastes. A very few W07s were built in right hand drive form.

Ferdinand Porsche had left Daimler-Benz in 1928 and his place as chief designer had been filled by the appointment of Hans Nibel, but quite a lot of what went into the Grosser Mercedes was probably first thought out by Porsche.

Nibel, as head of design, favoured the straight-eight engine, as would be fitted to the next generation of Mercedes sporting cars, the 380, 500 and 540K, rather than the six-cylinder cars designed by Professor Porsche. Nibel was seeking extra flexibility and smoothness of running in these big cars and believed that Mercedes achieved this with the M07, the designation given to the 7,665cc engine (hence the 770 name also given to the Typ W07) that was fitted to the W07. Initially, the car could be ordered with or without a supercharger but it would appear that very few were delivered without one. Incidentally, Daimler-Benz changed their Typ numbering system in 1937 and from then one, for one short year, the car was referred to as the Typ W107.

In 1930, at the London and Paris motor shows, and then at the Berlin show in 1931, Daimler-Benz had this to say in their first sales catalogue that was printed in English:

> The Grosser Mercedes is the car for those men of all countries who, satisfied only by the highest degree of efficiency in all that surrounds them, need a car, big not only in dimensions, but justifying to the full the more subtle implications of the word. Once again, the Daimler-Benz Works have created

Hitler on his way to the Siemens factory to deliver a speech on 10 November 1933 in a Mercedes-Benz W07 Grosser 770. (*Polish National Archives*)

> for the connoisseur a new automobile, which may justifiably lay claim to pride of place among the fine cars of the World – The Mercedes Super Straight Eight with or without supercharger, with low built chassis frame. Much which hitherto had remained unsolved has in this model received solution. Elegance, internal and external, here blends with luxurious comfort to form a car of unprecedented appeal.

The cylinder block of the engine was made of nickel-chromium-enforced cast iron, while the sump, crankcase and valve cover were in aluminium. The camshaft was positioned on the left side of the block, looking forward, and via pushrods and tappets, drove two valves per cylinder. The camshaft ran in nine plain bearings. Incidentally, it does seem surprising that Mercedes-Benz, having via Ferdinand Porsche pioneered the use of a single overhead camshaft

Hitler in one of his Mercedes Typ W08 'Grosser' 770s during a parade through Nuremberg in September 1935. Hitler used this Voll and Ruhrbeck bodied Mercedes-Benz extensively from 1931–1936. (*NARA*)

to operate the valves, should have regressed somewhat in designing a car with a side-mounted camshaft, operating the valves via pushrods. However, high rpm was not the object with the new Grosser, so perhaps pushrod-operated valve gear was seen as a simpler option?

Reich Chancellor Adolf Hitler (standing) with, behind him, the Vice-Chancellor Franz von Papen (seated), arriving at a ceremony on 1 May 1934. They are travelling in a Munich-registered Typ W07 Grosser 770 which was much used by Hitler at this time. (*Polish National Archives*)

The Roots-type supercharger was mounted on the right side of the engine and was driven from the crankshaft, via a clutch, which was activated when the driver pushed the accelerator pedal to the floor. The ignition system was normally by two distributors, with a magneto, or a distributor plus coil, driven from the dynamo. Whichever system was used, it powered two spark plugs per cylinder. The large starter motor was situated on the right side of the engine.

The crankshaft was of nickel-chromium steel, machined all over, with forged counterweights. Nine white metal bearings supported it in the crankcase. It drove the camshaft via helical gears. The Nelson-Bohnalite aluminium pistons each had one oil scraper and three plain rings. To ensure sufficient lubrication, three oil scavenge pumps were used and the water pump was driven from the fan shaft. The fan itself was easily removable for when running in cold weather.

The supercharger was driven via its own clutch, which was immersed in a bath of oil from the crankshaft and when engaged blew through the updraught, Mercedes-made, twin-choke carburettor. The manual recommended the supercharger not be used for longer than twenty seconds. The cast iron exhaust manifold was mounted on the right-hand side of the engine and above the inlet manifold, which was made of aluminium. This exhaust manifold had two exits for the exhaust itself, which was then piped through twin chromed pipes, which exited from the bonnet side and led to the exhaust system, mounted underneath the car and exiting at the rear.

Adolf Hitler, again in his Munich-registered Mercedes Typ W07 Grosser 770 during the same parade as above, through Nuremberg in September 1935. (*Polish National Archives*)

To transmit the power that this large engine produced, some 200bhp when the supercharger was engaged, 150 without, there was a twin-plate clutch and a three-speed gearbox. Overdrive could be specified by the owner when ordering his (or her) new car. This then would give the driver the choice of six forward speeds. There were two final drive ratios available to the customer: 4.5 or 4.9:1.

The rear axle was sprung on semi-elliptical leaf springs that, depending upon the car's weight, could be of 9, 10, 14, 15, or 16 leaves. The prop shaft from the rear axle to the gearbox/overdrive was encased in its own tube.

The solid front axle was made of nickel-chromium steel and the kingpins ran in roller bearings at the top and ball bearings at the bottom. Either Houdaille PLA or Walex Gabriel triple dampers were fitted. Front springs, like the rears, were semi-elliptical. Steering was by worm and nut.

All these mechanical parts were mounted into a chassis, which was composed of U-shaped steel side members, which kicked up slightly over the front springs, and more so at the rear axle position, to keep the centre of gravity low. There were five cross braces between these two side members, with the two rear engine mountings bolted directly to the side members to give added rigidity. Braking was by mechanically operated drum brakes, each one cast with cooling fins around its circumference, a fairly conventional system for the time. Either wooden or wire-spoked wheels of 20in in diameter by 7in wide could be specified, although the wooden-spoked wheels went out of fashion during the Grosser's production run in favour of wire wheels. The rear-mounted fuel tank held 120 litres, which included 8 litres in reserve. Lubrication of the chassis was provided for by engine oil from the sump every 62 miles.

Later on in the production run, the W07 was provided with a built-in hydraulic jack system, which saved the chauffeur performing the strenuous task of jacking up the heavy vehicle.

On the dashboard were the following instruments: temperature gauge, voltmeter, electric clock, tachometer, fuel gauge, ammeter, oil pressure gauge, and a speedometer, marked in kph. The steering wheel had on it a ring that, when pressed, sounded the horn, a button in the middle of the wheel that controlled the dimming of the headlights, and three more levers, which controlled the overdrive, the ignition and the richness or leanness of the fuel mixture.

The weight of the bare chassis, according to the factory, was 1,980kg (4,356lb), while the complete car, in Offener Tourenwagen Cabriolet F form, weighed 2,950kg (6,490lb), and could carry a payload of 520kg (1,144lb). Even fully loaded, maximum speed was given as 160kph (99.2mph), and factory records say that 117 chassis were delivered to bodybuilders, most being bodied at the Mercedes-Benz

Hitler and his chauffeur, Julius Schreck, in an official Mercedes prior to 1936. (*Historic Military Press*)

factory at Sindelfingen, near Stuttgart, where the company produced their car bodies among other products.

This factory had been in existence since 1915, producing aircraft during the First World War. By 1932, it was having serious financial and labour problems but with Hitler's accession to power, promising a new autobahn network and the abolition of registration taxes, more jobs needed to be filled in order to satisfy demand for new Mercedes-Benz cars, of which the Grosser was but one model. The Mercedes-Benz factory at Mannheim built just one Grosser body.

In 1933 1,200 jobs were created at the start of the year at Sindelfingen and another 3,000 workers had been taken on by December. Another 800 were hired in 1935. Among this workforce, only the most highly skilled were employed to work on the bodies of the Grosser.

The unclothed chassis were bodied with Pullman Limousine, with a glass partition in between the front and rear seats, or as Innenlinkers (short for Innensteuer-Limousine, a saloon body), or as 'Offener Tourenwagen' (open touring car). The Grossers, both W07 and the later W150, also came as the Cabriolet D, this seating for five people, or the Cabriolet F, seating six to seven people. Incidentally, the

Adolf Hitler's car is mobbed by a crowd on the day he was appointed to the office of the Reich Chancellor, 30 January 1933. (*Polish National Archives*)

President Paul von Hindenburg and Reich Chancellor Hitler approach an official Mercedes-Benz Typ W08 Grosser 770, from the Reichschancellery Motor Pool, at an event in Berlin on 1 May 1933. (*Historic Military Press*)

Offener Tourenwagen even featured a separate windshield, mounted above the central dividing position, to help keep the wind out of the hair of the passengers seated in the rear when the top was down.

Foreign coach builders for the W07 included Castagna in Italy, Lajos Zupka in Hungary and Rollston in the USA. Mercedes-Benz's special order department, the Sonderwagenbau, oversaw the W07s built for ex-Kaiser Wilhelm II and the Japanese Emperor. The one that went to Emperor Hirohito was a specially armoured version.

Several W07 Grossers were fitted with armour plating when they were built for various dignitaries around the world and, using the Aktion P (P for Panzerung, meaning armour), programme, later on during the war years and in that configuration, could weigh up to 4,540kg (9,980lb, or almost 5 tons fully loaded).

Prices for the W07 Grosser Mercedes, up to 1936, were RM 47,500 for a Cabriolet, whether B, D or F, RM 44,500 for a Cabriolet C (two windows, two doors, four seats), RM 42,000 for an Offener Tourenwagen (open tourer, six windows, four doors, seven or eight seats), RM 41,000 for a Pullman saloon (six windows, four doors, seven or eight seats), and RM 32,500 for a rolling chassis.

Grosser bodies were built mainly of steel, on a wooden frame, either of beech or ash, seasoned in the special sheds for this purpose at Sindelfingen. The Grosser chassis were not built on a production line, but were all hand built in the factory at Untertürkheim. The completed chassis then received their bodies from the bodybuilding plant at Sindelfingen, to which they had been transported on specially constructed trucks, to have their bodies mounted on the chassis, finished and painted. The completed cars were then test driven before final inspection to spot any defects and were only then delivered to the customer.[9]

Dignitaries lined up to welcome Hitler, who has arrived in one of his official Mercedes W07 Grosser, in about 1937. Note the imposing radiator and the third headlight. (*Polish National Archives*)

Erich Kempka wrote about the care with which he ordered the cars and his trips to the factory to oversee them being built: 'It was always my pleasure to watch over the new vehicles as they were being manufactured. Under my supervision and in close co-operation with the Daimler-Benz factory not only were the well-known Führer-cars built but also cross-country vehicles for manoeuvres, later used for drives in the mountains and later still well proven during the war.'[10]

One hundred and seventeen W07/107s were built between 1930 and 1938, with some being sold to dignitaries from abroad, including King Faisal I of Iraq, Pope Pius XI and Hirohito, Emperor of Japan. Noted German customers included the abdicated Kaiser Wilhelm II, then living in the Netherlands, and the Chancellor before Hitler, Paul von Hindenburg.

One of Mercedes-Benz's competitors to the new Grosser was Maybach, with their DS (Doppel Sechs/Double Six), DS7 Zeppelin. This had a V12 engine of 6,971cc, which produced 150hp at a lowly 2,800rpm. It actually pre-dated Mercedes-Benz's Grosser by a year, first appearing in 1929. Known first of all as the Maybach 12, it was reintroduced as the DS8 Zeppelin in 1930; from 1930 the V12 engine was enlarged to 7,977cc and now produced 200hp at 3,200rpm. The car itself was so heavy, at 6,600lb, that the driver (presumably the chauffeur for this very expensive car) had to have not only a licence to drive a car, but also a truck driver's licence. A maximum speed of 108mph was claimed for this behemoth.

The main competitor in the very top end of the luxury car market was, of course, Rolls-Royce. In 1929, just the year before the W07 Grosser 770 had been introduced, the British manufacturer had brought out their new prestigious car, the Phantom II. This followed on from the original Phantom, a design still using the chassis from the previous Silver Ghost, which had had a straight-six engine.

The new Phantom II not only had a newer, lower chassis, still with leaf spring suspension and beam axles all round, but it also had a new engine with overhead valves in a detachable cylinder head of aluminium. This engine was, strangely enough, very much the same size as the W07 Grosser, 7,668cc. Rolls-Royce did not release their engine performance figures, simply using the old RAC tax system of referring to the Phantom II as: '40/50'. Whatever the power (and it must have been in excess of 120bhp), this was transmitted to the rear axle by a new four-speed gearbox. The chassis featured central lubrication and the brakes, on all four wheels, were Servo-assisted. The whole car weighed some 6,600lb.

Bodies for the Phantom were built by, among others, Mulliner, Park Ward, Hooper, Carolton, Thrupp and Maberly, Brewster, and Barker. Top of the line of this prestigious car was the new Continental, with a shorter than standard wheelbase at 144in and stiffer than standard springing. All the cars were built at the Rolls-Royce factory at Derby, England. In one area the Rolls-Royce was the clear victor: Sales. Total production of the Phantom II was 1,281 cars between 1929 and 1936, which included 281 Continentals.

In America, the only real choice for the customer who wanted any US-built car that could compete with the W07 Grosser was the Duesenberg Models J and SJ but only a handful were built. Cadillac brought out their V16, with its 7.4-litre engine, but later said that they had lost money on every one of the around 4,076 cars built over the ten-year production run of 1930 to 1940.

Hitler appeared in several Grosser W07s, right from the time that they were announced. His first appearance in one was in 1931 on 11 October. He insisted on standing on a raised platform, which stood above the actual front passenger seat by 13cm, so that he could be seen by and wave to the crowds.

Hitler at the IV Olympic Winter Games in Garmisch-Partenkirchen in February 1936, in a Mercedes-Benz W24 540 Fahrzeug Lang. (*Polish National Archives*)

Hitler is more frequently seen in 1932 and 1933 in a Voll and Ruhrbeck-bodied W07 Offener Tourenwagen with the Munich registration IIA-19357. Hitler used it several times in 1933, culminating when he opened the Nazi Party rally in Nuremberg in September.[11]

There are photos extant of Hitler travelling, in his usual position in the front passenger space, on parade in a Mercedes-Benz Typ W08 Nürburg 460 in the early 1930s. The immatriculation/registration number of this car was 11A-22006. This was another Ferdinand Porsche design, originally in 1928 with a side valve eight-cylinder inline engine, and it had been aimed originally as a competitor to the Paul Daimler-designed Horch 8, but it had not initially been a success. The W08 Nürburg 460 was substantially revised for 1929 after Dr Porsche left Mercedes-Benz.

Principally, the new design of the chassis went from one being mounted on top of the beam axles to one being mounted underneath the axles, to give a lower look and improve road holding. A golden figure '8' embedded in a lozenge shape adorns the owner's manual of these cars.

The Nürburg name came from the fact that in a test run, one of the prototypes of this car had been driven non-stop at the Nürburgring for thirteen days and nights, covering 20,000km, and averaging a speed of 64kph.

The engine of the 1929 car was very much the same as the 1928 model, a straight-eight design with side valves, non-supercharged, of 4,622cc. Its maximum power was 79bhp and maximum speed was just 62mph when the car was first introduced in 1928. There was a four-speed gearbox without synchromesh, and the car could also be ordered with an overdrive. The weight of the Offener Tourenwagen was 2,150kg. It was, at the time, comfortably outsold by its competitor from Horch.

In 1931, the engine was enlarged to 4,918cc and the power now increased to 99bhp, with the maximum speed going up to 69mph. For 1962, the Nürburg name was dropped; now the car was simply referred to as the Typ 500. With a few transmission ratio changes, the car could reach 75mph. Its wheelbase came in two lengths, 3,430mm and 3,670mm, and the later 500N had an engine of 4918cc giving 100–110bhp. That car appears to have been available from the factory with a wheelbase of 3,670mm. This model was not officially available until later as the 19/100hp Nürburg 500.[12] Both cars were unsupercharged, hence the lack of the distinctive 'K' for Kompressor after the Type numerals.

Hitler was photographed in one such car on 8 October 1934, leading a convoy of similar vehicles. Once again, the car that he was travelling in wore the immatriculation/registration plate 11A-22006. A very similar car was seen in Berlin in 1935, again with Hitler riding in it. At least two more Nürburg 500 Offener Tourenwagens were in use by the government during 1935/36. As late as

Adolf Hitler, heading a parade, in a Typ 460 Nurburgring, in 1931/32. (*Polish National Archives*)

1943, Mussolini was transported to Hitler's headquarters in a Nürburg 500 Offener Tourenwagen, immatriculation number 1A-148 543.[13]

Julius Schreck died of meningitis in May 1936. Hitler was very upset by this and ordered a Nazi state funeral for him. His place was taken by twenty-six-year-old Erich Kempka. Already a Nazi Party member from 1930, Kempka had previously been a car mechanic with DKW, so he had a very good working knowledge of vehicles. He had then been a chauffeur to Josef Terboven, the Oberpraesident of Prussia's Rheinprovinz. He was another ex-First World War soldier who had joined the Nazi Party. Terboven recommended Kempka to Hitler as a chauffeur early in 1932.

Nevertheless, Kempka still had to attend an interview with Hitler, with several other candidates, plus a final meeting with him before his appointment was confirmed.

Accepted for that post, he would also be named as one of the eight original members of Hitler's bodyguard – the SS-Begleitkommando.

As Hitler's chauffeur, Kempka journeyed right across Germany. Indeed, as he related, his first action after his appointment was to jump into the Führer's 6-litre

Adolf Hitler during a visit to Vienna in October 1938 in a new Mercedes-Benz Typ W150 Grosser 770. Erich Kempka, his regular chauffeur from 1936, is at the wheel. (*Polish National Archives*)

Mercedes and drive the 480 or so kilometres from Munich to Berlin. In his book *I was Hitler's Chauffeur*, Kempka described what driving for Hitler was like:

> In 1932 I drove 132,000 kilometres, crossing all over Germany by day and night. My life was enriched on these trips by many experiences. I never had the feeling of being on travels with a 'boss', but rather with an elder, fatherly friend. He rarely spoke to me about politics, but said I could and should come to him with my personal problems and needs. He had an understanding and a ready ear for everything. He would always ensure that we drivers had the best accommodation and food on the way, emphasizing: 'My drivers and pilots are my best friends! I entrust my life to these men!'

Kempka recounted in his book that to wash and clean properly a Grosser Mercedes took some four hours.[14]

A Mercedes-Benz W07 Grosser 770 Offener Tourenwagen in the Mercedes-Benz Museum in Stuttgart in 1971. This may have been the car delivered to Kaiser Wilhelm II in Holland. (*Photo courtesy of Carl de Bickero*)

Where road tests of the W07 were concerned, *Auto Motor und Sport* wrote that: 'The Grosser's top speed is comparable to a racecar,' and:

> Whilst it would be unwise to exceed 70kph with other cars of the same category, there are no limits with this Mercedes. We do not know of any car that allows you to drive at such a high level of safety, at such breathtaking speeds and in such exceptional comfort. The existence of such a car for Daimler-Benz, in our view, is an illustration of what can be done best with today's means.
>
> In contrast to the American view, which is in favour of the V-engine of the twelve- or sixteen-cylinder type as far as representatives of this price category are concerned, they have remained remarkably sober in giving the Super Mercedes an eight-cylinder in-line engine. With a vehicle whose fundamental tendency is towards exclusivity to such a great extent they thought that any excursion into uncharted waters would be fatal. That is how the new design from Daimler-Benz came to be a happy avowal of traditional links.
>
> We know of vehicles, even more recent ones, in which it would be reckless to drive at over 70km/h, whereas there is no such limit where the Super Mercedes is concerned. In contrast to some statements made by the competition which

Hitler reviews a parade from an open-top Mercedes W07 Grosser in about September 1937. (*Polish National Archives*)

> have come to light, the conduct of the Super Mercedes at all speeds is beyond reproach. Whilst the car's springing is not as sensitive as it is amongst the American competitors, the Super Mercedes enables a sure driving style that secures cohesion with the road. We do not know of any vehicle that would allow such safe driving with heavy bodies at the breathtaking speed of 120 km/h. And this is probably where the ultimate sense and the ultimate justification for the existence of this vehicle model are to be found. In spite of its orthodox fundamental philosophy, the Super Mercedes presents itself as the worthy conclusion of Daimler-Benz production and as the final enhancement of automotive comfort achievable with today's means.

However, the magazine did have some criticism to make about the springing:

> The rather unpleasant lateral swaying of the body would be dealt with by strengthening the slightly soft springs and by tightening the shock absorbers and would then probably cease; however the question remains whether the springing would be sufficient on poor rural roads – which predominate on long journeys – to retain the high average. As is the case with the new twelve-cylinder Maybach, it is very apparent here that future work must concentrate on improving the handling.[15]

The editor of the *Allgemeine Zeitung* wrote: 'With this model the German automobile industry regains its place, at the highest level and at the forefront of this very exclusive segment in which it has excelled since the beginning of the automobile. The tone is set: eleven years after the treaty of Versailles, Greater Germany is back!'

Hitler can be seen in a W07 Grosser Mercedes-Benz in many photographs from late 1931 onwards. Indeed, it was not until the advent of the W24 540K Lang in 1936 that he travelled officially in any other car except a few occasions when he was seen in a Typ W08 Nürburg 460 or 500. Hitler had at least eight W07 Grosser Offener Tourenwagens in the squadron of cars that was always kept at his disposal in the ReichsKanzelerei Motor Pool in Berlin and at the Berghof. All six of the W24s built were used by the Reich Motor Pool too.[16]

In 1931, Hitler was involved as a passenger in another car accident. On 23 December that year, the *New York Times*, quoting the AP agency reported:

> Kyritz, Germany, Dec 22: Adolf Hitler, head of the German Fascists, suffered a broken finger today in an automobile accident. The car ahead of his skidded into a tree at the side of a country road not far from here and Hitler's machine, in which General Von App was a passenger, struck the first car.

Adolf Hitler in one of the Reichchancellery Motor Pool's Mercedes-Benz Typ W08 Grosser 770s in Berlin on 1 May 1935. (*Historic Military Press*)

The Rev. Wenzel, who recently officiated at the marriage of Joseph Goebbels, National Socialist leader, received a broken nose. The driver of the other car was taken to hospital with a fractured skull.[17]

Whichever type of car Hitler had been travelling in was not mentioned it but may have been the Nürburg 460 that he tended to use at this time.

In February 1932, the SS-Begleitkommando des Führers ('escort command of the Führer'), SSBKdF for short, was formed. This was a small group of eight men, solely tasked with protecting Hitler. From this unit were drawn the men who always accompanied Hitler in his car. The original members were: Erich Kempka, Adolf Dirr, August Korber, Kurt Gildisch, Bruno Gesche, Bodo Gelzenleuchter, Willi Herzberger and Franz Schadle.[18]

The SS man who sat immediately behind Hitler always jumped out of the car as it was coming to a halt, in order to open the Führer's door for him. The other SS man in the back seat had a machine pistol, in case of severe trouble.

Riding in an 'Offener Tourenwagen' (open-touring car) Munich registered Mercedes-Benz, Typ W24 540 Fahrzeug Lang, (Long chassis), Adolf Hitler passes through the crowds on his way to the IV Olympic Winter Games in Garmisch-Partenkirchen in February 1936. (*Polish National Archives*)

Chancellor Adolf Hitler and President Paul von Hindenburg in an official car, pause while a boy gives Hitler a lapel badge, in August 1934. (*Danish National Museum*)

The Weimar Republic, the federal constitutional republic that had governed Germany since 1918, was tottering. By now the great depression had set in after the Wall Street crash of 1929 and unemployment had spread across the world, with the German government using a policy of deflation to attempt to balance the economy but this only encouraged unemployment and was setting the scene for the Nazis rise to power. Chancellor Heinrich Brüning, backed by President Paul von Hindenburg's use of emergency powers, promoted this policy but it was not enough to halt the slide into insolvency of Germany. One of the policy's side effects was to cut the amount of unemployment benefits.

In 1931, Britain devalued the pound by leaving the gold standard, and this affected many other countries, primarily leaving British-made goods some 20 per cent cheaper than those of Germany. Germany, despite managing to negotiate a halt to its reparation payments, had to reduce its prices by the same to remain competitive and this resulted in even more benefit cuts. The government resigned and there was a general election, which saw the vote for the NSDAP rise five-fold.

During spring 1932 there were 6 million people unemployed in Germany and many citizens were facing ruin, homelessness and starvation. Suddenly, Hitler seemed like a saviour to millions of them.[19]

On 13 March 1932 there was a presidential election and Hitler received over 11 million votes, only 30 per cent of the total. Hindenburg, the incumbent, received over 18 million votes. This meant that there would be a run-off election and Hitler saw his opportunity, urging Goebbels on to another strong campaign for the 10 April poll.

Hitler partook in a very strenuous campaign, attending many rallies and once again giving speeches to as many people as possible. He used his Junkers Ju 52/3m three-engined aircraft to fly many miles and to put across a very positive message, promising a better life for Germans. 'In the Third Reich every German girl will find a husband!' Hitler told the crowds. President Hindenburg did not take part in a campaign, leaving it to the German people to make up their minds between him and Hitler. In the run-off election itself, Hitler once again increased his share of the vote, without gaining the absolute majority needed and while Hindenburg remained president, it was obvious that Hitler and the Nazis were now the party on the march.

In the late spring 1932 there were over 400,000 stormtroopers in the Nazi Party and Adolf Hitler had to rein in their violence from time to time, as he had his own plans on how to gain power. In April, the Chancellor of Germany, Heinrich Brüning, banned the SA and the SS. Hitler agreed, as he realised that the Chancellorship of Germany was within his grasp. Brüning resigned on 29 May.

There were many political machinations taking place in Germany in 1932 and by July there was violence on the streets, with shootings and beatings. Martial law was declared in Berlin.

More political machinations ensued and Hitler succeeded in fomenting a war of intrigue between Kurt von Schleicher, an ex-army officer with pretensions of adequacy to lead Germany, and Franz von Papen, who had succeeded Brüning.

Yet another general election took place in July, the result of which was that the Nazi Party gained 230 seats in the Reichstag. They were now the most powerful party in Germany.

Hitler attending a parade in Berlin in 1936, the occasion being the anniversary of his appointment as Chancellor. (*Historic Military Press*)

On 13 August, Schleicher and von Papen denied Hitler his right to become Chancellor and Hitler threatened to unleash the SA for three days across Germany to foment violent revolt. However, in an interview with Hindenburg, he revoked this order. November saw Hindenburg again refusing, twice, to make Hitler Chancellor of Germany.

But now fate took a turn. The industrialists and bankers of Germany, including Krupp and I.G. Farben, petitioned Hindenburg to grant Hitler the Chancellorship. The Army high command also wanted Hitler as a leader, as they saw that he would throw off the shackles of the Treaty of Versailles.

Hindenburg, not wanting Hitler to become Chancellor, in the end backed von Schleicher, on 2 December 1932. The problem was, von Schleicher was now not trusted by any of the powers in Germany to work honestly with von Papen in a coalition. Von Schleicher resigned on 28 January 1933.

On 30 January, Hindenburg met Hitler and appointed him Reich Chancellor of all Germany. Suddenly, Hitler had achieved his ambition and shortly afterwards dissolved the Reichstag and declared himself 'Der Führer', dictator of all Germany.[20]

Among Hitler's first decrees upon taking power were the abolition of registration taxes/charges upon buying a new car, and the announcement of the building of the autobahns. These announcements supercharged the demand for new and better cars. The industry moved towards full production.

Hitler's income in 1933 was 1,232,335 Marks. Hitler owed 405,494 Marks in tax for 1933 and the advance payment for 1934. However, the Reich President, Hindenburg, died on 2 August 1934 and Hitler immediately declared himself President through the enabling act, even though the German constitution forbade it. As the office of President was exempt from all taxes, the little matter of Hitler's tax debt was conveniently overlooked.[21]

A little-known fact is that when Hitler became Chancellor, and then dictator of Germany, all the then employed police were required to become members of the SS, which included having their SS numbers tattooed onto their arms. A number of such police were transferred into a new security service in 1933, charged, like the Führerbegleitkommando, with guarding the personal safety of Hitler. They were known as the Reichssicherheitsdienst, or RSD for short.

On the evening of 5 March, Hitler dined with the Army General Staff and informed them that he intended that they should conquer 'lands to the east'.[22]

Now, with public finances from taxpayers' money available to him, Hitler promptly ordered ten W07 Grosser Mercedes Offener Tourenwagens for the Reich Chancellery motor pool. He could now take his pick from whichever one was available.

Mercedes-Benz Typ W08 460 Nürburg 18/80

Manufacturer

1928–39:	Daimler-Benz A.G.
Type:	1928–39: Mercedes W08/W108
Built in:	Stuttgart, Germany
Body and chassis:	Either an Offener Tourenwagen (open tourer), or a Limousine (enclosed sedan), or a Landaulet (4-door cabriolet). The car could also be purchased as a rolling chassis and a body built/bought separately.

Engine

Bore × stroke:	78mm × 115mm
	Eight cylinders inline, 4624cc, side valves, unsupercharged
Max. Power:	90bhp @ 3,100rpm

Max. Speed:	120kph
Range:	400km
Gearbox:	4 forward speeds plus reverse and optional overdrive
Brakes:	Servo-assisted drums all round

Suspension

Front:	Beam axle, semi-elliptic springs
Rear:	Live axle, semi-elliptic springs

Dimensions

Wheelbase:	3,670mm
Front track:	1,485mm
Rear track:	1,485mm
Tyre Size:	6.50-20

Mercedes-Benz Typ W08 500 19/100 Nürburg

Manufacturer

1932–39:	Daimler-Benz A.G.

Type

1928–38:	Mercedes W08/W108
Built in:	Stuttgart, Germany
Chassis:	Boxed ladder frame
Body:	Either an Offener Tourenwagen (open tourer), or a Limousine (enclosed sedan), or a Landaulet (4-door cabriolet). The car could also be purchased as a rolling chassis and a body built separately by a coach builder.

Engine

Bore × stroke:	82.5mm × 115mm
	Eight cylinders inline, 4918cc, side valves, unsupercharged
Max. Power:	90bhp @ 3,100rpm
Max. Speed:	120kph
Range:	400km
Gearbox:	4 forward speeds plus reverse and optional overdrive
Brakes:	Servo-assisted drums all round

Suspension

Front:	Beam axle, semi elliptic springs
Rear:	Live axle, semi-elliptic springs

Dimensions

Standard Wheelbase:	3,670mm
Short wheelbase:	3,430mm
Front track:	1,485mm
Rear track:	1,485mm
Tyre Size:	6.50-20
Width:	1,820mm
Height:	1,820mm

Reg/Immatric No: **1A-111**
Berlin registered
W07 Grosser 770K
Offener Tourenwagen
Ministry of Propaganda
Used by Goebbels

Reg/Immatric No: **1A-16916**
Berlin registered
W07 Grosser 770K
Offener Tourenwagen
Hitler used
1937: 29 September: Mussolini visit. Back-up car

Reg/Immac no: **Z-57501**
W07 Grosser 770K
Offener Tourenwagen
Used by Hitler
1935: January: Berlin
1936: March: Essen
June: Olympic Village, Berlin

Reg/Immac no: **11A-19351**
Munich registered
W07 Grosser 770K
Offener Tourenwagen
Used by Hitler

Reg/Immac no: **IIA-19356**
Munich registered

W07. Grosser 770K
RSD. Offener Tourenwagen. Voll & Ruhrbeck bodied
Used by Hitler

1934:	1 May: Ceremonial Rally, with Vice Chancellor von Papen
1935:	September: Nuremberg Nazi Party Rally
1936:	20 April: Hitler's birthday
	1 August: Parade before Olympic Games start
	13 September: SA Parade, Nuremburg
1938:	6 April: Hitler to Salzburg, Austria
	8 April: Parade in Vienna
	??: Konigstrasse, Stuttgart
1939:	20 April: Hitler's birthday. Support car
1940:	6 July: Security car for Hitler's motorcade

Reg/Immac no: **11A-19357**
Munich registered
W07 Grosser. 770K
Offener Tourenwagen. Voll & Ruhrbeck bodied
Used by Hitler

1931:	On Parade with Hitler
1932:	August: Berlin parade with Hitler
1933:	September: Hitler/Röhm. Nuremberg party rally
	23 September: Hanover
	10 November: Speech at Siemens factory
1934:	20 April: Hitler's birthday parade
	May 1: Lustgarten, Berlin
	??: Leipzig
	4 September: Reich party day celebrations, Nuremberg
	8 September: Nuremberg
	9 September: SA Salute. Nuremburg
	30 September: Hildesheim
1935:	20 March: Bernsheim
	15 September: SA salute. Nuremburg?
1936:	9 September: Reviewing SA, Adolf Hitler Plaza
	Berlin. Hitler Jugend
	Autobahn opening

Reg/Immac no: **IIA-22006**
Munich registered
Offener Tourenwagen
Used by Hitler
First seen on a Nürburg 460 in the early 1930s with Hitler on parade
Then **IIA-22006** is seen on a later Nürburg 500, again with Hitler, on 8 October 1934. Then:

1935: **IIA-22006** now on a W07 Grosser. Possibly as each car is returned to the factory in a part-exchange deal, the registration number can be reused on a newer car?
1936: February: Winter Olympic Games, Garmisch-Partenkirchen, Germany
Autobahn opening

Reg/Immac no: **IIA-37305**
Munich registered
W07.Grosser 770K
Offener Tourenwagen
Used by Hitler
1937: 24 November: Anniversary of Nazi Party founding

Reg/Immac no: **IVB-75995**
W07. Grosser 770K
Offener Tourenwagen
Used by Hitler
1933: Pforzheim

Reg/Immac no: **1A-18387**
W07/107 Grosser 770K
Offener Tourenwagen
Used by Heinrich Himmler in 1936

Reg/Immac no: **IIA - 44962**
W107 Grosser 770K
Munich registered
Offener Tourenwagen
1938: 8/9 April: RSD escort car. Austria

Reg/Immac no: **IIIA-33912**
W07. Grosser 770K

Stuttgart registered
Offener Tourenwagen
Used by Herman Goering
1934: 24 April: Memorial service in Wesermünde. Goering

Reg/Immac no: **IVB-27014**
W07. Grosser 770K
Offener Tourenwagen
1934: September: Nazi Party congress, Nuremberg

Known chassis numbers:

1930 W07 770:
Chassis number: U83816
Engine number: 83816
Body style: Cabriolet D
In Imperial Palace Collection, Las Vegas, prior to 2000

1931 W07 770:
Chassis number: U83824
Engine number: 83824
Body style: Cabriolet D. Conv
In Imperial Palace Collection, Las Vegas, prior to 2000

1931 W07 770:
Chassis number: U85205
Engine number: 85205
Body style: Cabriolet D. Conv
In Imperial Palace Collection, Las Vegas, prior to 2000

1935 W07 770:
Chassis number: U85245
Engine number:
Body style: Cabriolet D. Conv
In Imperial Palace Collection, Las Vegas, prior to 2000

1935 W07 770:
Chassis number: U85245
Engine number:

Body style: Cabriolet D. Conv
In Imperial Palace Collection, Las Vegas, prior to 2000

1935 W07 770:
Chassis number: U85260
Engine number:
Body style: Cabriolet D
In Imperial Palace Collection, Las Vegas, prior to 2000

1937 W07 770:
Chassis number: U85270
Engine number: 85270
Body style: Pullman Limousine BP
In Imperial Palace Collection, Las Vegas, prior to 2000

1937 W07 770:
Chassis number: U85625
Engine number: 852625
Body style: Pullman Limousine
In Imperial Palace Collection, Las Vegas, prior to 2000

Chapter 5

Mercedes-Benz W24

By November 1931, the W07 Grosser 770 was well into production and, as a successor to both this and the Typ W08 Nürburg 460/500, Mercedes-Benz now looked at producing the W24. However, only six would be built in 1936–38 and all were bought and used by German government ministers, including, of course, Hitler. At this time, Mercedes had many different car models in production and it can be seen that the W24 was an attempt at a rationalisation of the catalogue. At the end of much discussion, it was decided by the management that a car with the same engine size as the W07 Grosser, but which produced even

Adolf Hitler salutes the ranks of German youth from his car during a Reichsparteitag, or Reich Party Day, parade in Nuremberg in September 1937. (*Danish National Museum*)

more power and torque, would also be designed and produced at a later stage. This would be the W150 Grosser 770 and it would replace the W07 Grosser 770 and the W24 540K Lang in 1938. We shall describe this car, of which Hitler used many, in a later chapter.[1]

In late 1934, at the Motor Show in London, a press release from Daimler-Benz outlined the general programme and outlook of the company:

> The especial value of the Mercedes-Benz programme of production does not only lie in the technical perfection and superior performance of its various models, but also in its extreme comprehensiveness, comprising as it does, a complete range of cars, commencing with a low-priced popular model and concluding with the representative automobiles of the big class, all of which comply in every respect with all the demands one can make upon a car; furthermore, this programme never deviates a hair's breadth from the guiding principle of providing absolutely first class material and the most highly developed workmanship obtainable.

Designed in 1934–35, the W24 used the M24 engine, itself a supercharged M24 5.4 litre straight-eight cylinder unit, then being an enlarged development of the engine that was powering the current 500K roadster, which became the revered 540K. Hans Nibel, the car's chief designer, had died suddenly in November 1934 and so Max Sailer took over his position and oversaw its design and development.

Called the 540 K Lang ('K' for Kompressor, or Supercharger, and 'Lang' for long wheelbase), the new W24 was both longer and wider than the Typ W07 Grosser, and had boxed-in chassis side rails for added torsional stiffness. The inside sections of the side chassis rails were heavily drilled in an attempt to lighten the chassis, which also had five cross members welded, not bolted, in place. The frame was bowed over the rear axle and also swept up at the front, to accommodate the beam front axle. This gave the effect of lowering the chassis around the driver and passenger compartment.

Springing of the front suspension was via semi-elliptical fore and aft leaf springs. The steering was a new design, featuring worm and nut operation. All four brake drums were hydraulically operated and either wood or wire wheels could be specified.

Effectively, the rear suspension was a De Dion arrangement (known internally at the factory as the 'parallel wheel arrangement'), whereby the half-shafts were connected at either end via U-joints and a tube ran beneath the differential, from one brake backplate to the other. There was another V-shaped arm running from the cross member behind the gearbox, linking up to the De Dion tube at the rear, on either side. This arrangement made sure that the rear axle could not move fore

Adolf Hitler on his way to open the Olympic Games in Berlin, on 1 August 1936, in his Munich-registered Mercedes-Benz Typ W34 Fahrzeug Lang Offentourenwagen. This, and the other Munich registered Mercedes-Benz cars were normally kept at Hitler's mountain retreat, in the Berghof, Obersalzburg, Bavaria. Note the swastika-bedecked Brandenberg gate behind him.

and aft, and also was firmly located side to side. Large coil springs at the rear worked in conjunction with the dampers, which were located within the tube that ran above the differential nose. Anti-roll bars were in use at both front and rear. A similar (though not identical) arrangement would be found on the Typ W150 Grosser of 1938.

The straight-eight M24 engine of 5.4 litres was very similar to that used in the 540K roadsters, featuring a crankshaft that was drop forged from nickel-chromium steel, with counterweights. The block and crankcase were of cast iron, as was the head, while the sump and valve cover were cast in aluminium. There were two valves per cylinder, operated by a camshaft set low in the block, operating pushrods that, in turn via rockers set in the top of the head, drove the valves up and down. Maximum rpm were 3,400.

The cast-iron exhaust manifold was mounted on the right-hand side of the engine and above the inlet manifold, which was made of aluminium. This exhaust manifold had two exits for the exhaust itself, like the 500K and 540Ks, which was then piped through twin chromed pipes. These exited from the bonnet side and led to the exhaust system, mounted underneath the car and exiting at the rear. These chromed exhaust pipes were to let onlookers know that this was a top-of-the range

Hitler in a Mercedes W24 in Cologne, 28 March 1936.

Mercedes-Benz. Horsepower was given, by the factory, as 115, with 180 being available when the supercharger was engaged. Top speed was 140kph (86.8mph).

A four-speed and reverse manual gearbox, operating via a single-plate clutch was used.

All six cars were bodied as Offener Tourenwagens and used, particularly by Hitler, as parade cars or by other members of the government for official business. Hitler was often seen in a W24, registered as 1A-103708, from November 1936 until April 1938, when he started using a W150 Grosser 770. Oddly, one of the W24s would have been preferred by Professor Oliveira Salazar, prime minister of Portugal, to the armoured W07 that he eventually received from Hitler.[2]

It is probable that when Sailer became head the design department, he most likely thought by July 1936 that the W24 design was not worth proceeding with. He likely judged that, with the new W150 design on the drawing board that would include such improvements as independent front suspension and a reversion to the bigger, 7.7-litre engine, which had powered the previous W07 Grosser Mercedes, this would completely overshadow the W24. He was right.

It was also during 1936 that Erich Kempka became Hitler's principal chauffeur. He later recounted:

> On the morning of 16 May 1936 I was summoned to Hitler's apartment on Prinz-Regenten-Strasse in Munich. I found him visibly sad and upset. Briefly

he informed me of the sudden death of his long-standing loyal companion Julius Schreck. I was appointed successor to Schreck with immediate effect. At the same time I was nominated head of the Führer's motor pool [Chef des Kraftfahrwesens des Führers] and promoted to SS-Sturmbannführer. All rights and duties of my predecessor were transferred to me.

The sudden death of Schreck affected me deeply. Ever since the first day, when he had given me such a kindly welcome, I had had much to thank him for. I knew nothing of the illness that befell him on a journey from Berlin to Munich. Immediately he arrived he had been hospitalized with severe meningitis, from which he died shortly afterwards. Fate had therefore afforded me no opportunity to take my leave of him.

For me there now began an exhausting period of special responsibility for someone of my fairly young age. I had to be constantly available for duty. I had hardly any free time for myself any more. The demands made of me grew ever larger. New vehicles had to be built. The garages were too small. Mechanics and other personnel had to be recruited. Additionally I had to keep up with the correspondence, which made demands on my time long after my official working day had ended. Hitler placed great personal trust in me, but he insisted that I complied with his requirements and deadlines precisely and to the letter. This trust was naturally a great stimulant for my ambitions.[3]

W24 540K Lang specification

Cubic Capacity:	5.4 litres
Cylinders:	8
Bore × Stroke:	88 × 111mm
Max. bhp:	115 Unsupercharged, 180 supercharged
Max RPM:	3,400
Valve gear:	Overhead valves, with pushrods
Wheelbase:	3,880mm
Front track:	1,535mm
Rear track:	1,547mm
Tyre Size:	7.50 × 17
Gearbox/speeds:	4-speed with synchromesh on 2nd, 3rd, 4th gear
Front suspension:	Beam
Rear suspension:	Swing axle w/anti-roll bar
Brakes:	Hydraulic
Max. speed:	140kph
Range:	500km

Reg/Immatriculation no: **1A-103708.** Berlin Olympics: Hitler in 'Experimental W24 Offener Tourenwagen (open touring car)'. 5.4-litre straight 8. Factory referred to it as: '540K long chassis'.

1936: Berlin Motor Show
1937: Hitler on parade
29 September: Mussolini visit. Hitler
1938: 18 February: Opening of Berlin Motor Show
16 March: Hitler in Munich
8/9 April: Linz: Hitler used. Parade through Austria, inc. Klagenfurt
May: Mayday Parade. Hitler

NOTE: **1A-103708.** This number was then transferred onto a W150 Grosser Mercedes and used by Hitler. Original car returned to factory and scrapped/reduced to parts?

Reg/Immatriculation no: **IA-139941**. W24, '540K Long Chassis'. Offener Tourenwagen.

1939: On Parade. Goring
1940: Paris. Goring. Visit to German Embassy

Reg/Immatriculation no: **11A-48234**. W24, '540K Long Chassis'. Offener Tourenwagen.
Hitler

1937: 14 May: Augsburg Theatre
September: Augsburg Parade with Hitler and Mussolini
9 November: Munich

Reg/Immatriculation no: **11A-56388**. W24, '540K Long Chassis'. Offener Tourenwagen.

1938: August: Nuremburg parade

Reg/Immatriculation no: **11B-120124**. Possibly a W24, '540K Long Chassis'. Offener Tourenwagen.

1937: Autobahn opening parade

Chapter 6

Mercedes-Benz 770 Grosser W150, 1938–44

The reason that the Typ W24 540K Lang project was dropped was because Mercedes-Benz already had a newer, more futuristic replacement for the W07 on the drawing board in 1936.

This was the new W150 Grosser, which, although from the outside it looked very similar to the old W07 (now renumbered in 1937 under the new numbering system at Mercedes-Benz as the Typ W107), was a quantum leap ahead in its designer's

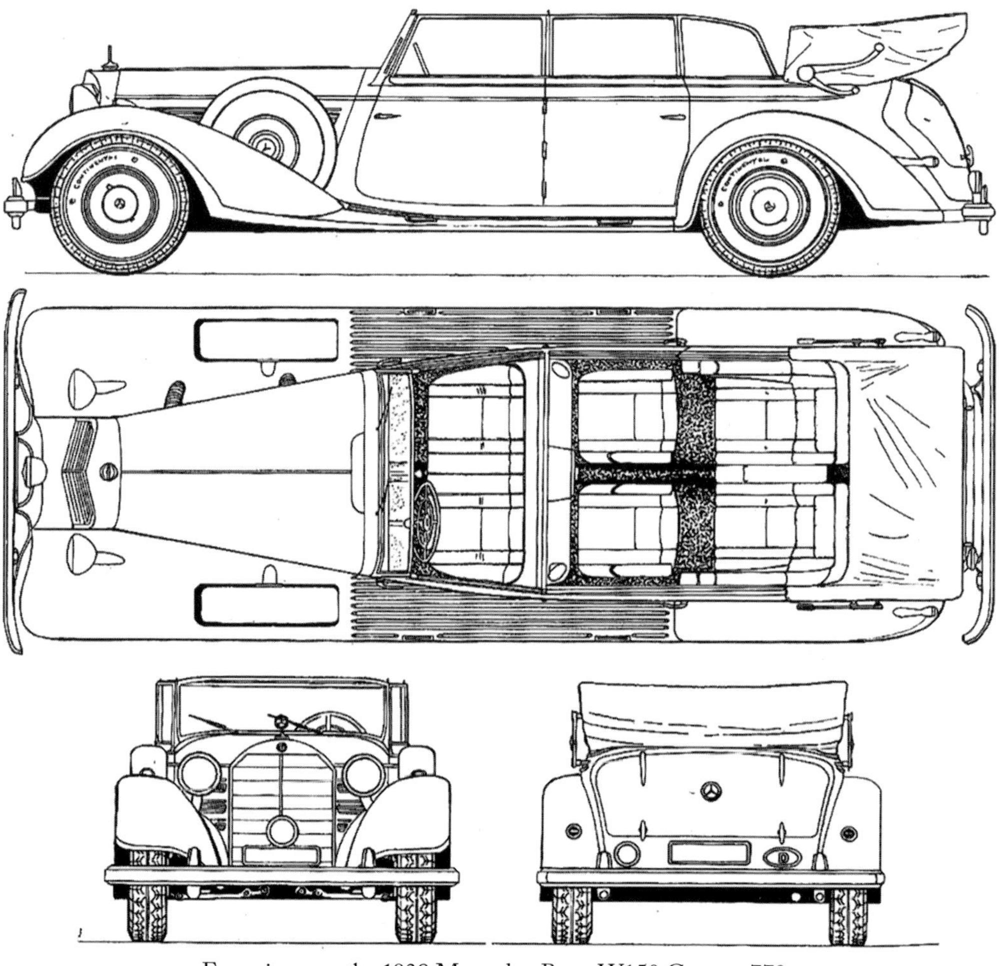

Four views on the 1938 Mercedes-Benz W150 Grosser 770.

thinking about the chassis and suspension design and had better riding qualities than the old W07/W107 Grosser. The people in charge of design of the W150 Grosser were those intimately connected with the racing side of Mercedes-Benz: Max Sailer and Max Wagner.[1]

For a start, there was the new chassis. No longer made the old way, with U-shaped chassis side and cross members bolted together, this was now built of oval tubular steel members, all welded together, to give a much stiffer chassis than the old design. It was also wider and longer than the old design, 1,650mm for the rear track instead of the previous 1,500mm and 3,880mm long for the wheelbase, as against the W07's 3,750mm.

The other major departure from the old W07's design would be in the front suspension. This new Grosser Mercedes would not have the old-style beam axle, its suspension would be fully independent, as on the Typ 540K design.

The decision to go with a completely new design had been made by Daimler-Benz in 1936. Indeed, they had promised the public that the prototype would be displayed at the 1938 Berlin Motor Show to be held in February 1938. The board kept to their word and the bare rolling chassis was exhibited, as promised, but needed to return to the factory afterwards to receive its new body.

The chassis itself had six oval tubular steel cross members (one of them going through the gearbox casing to give added rigidity in the middle of the chassis), and was developed from the experience Mercedes designers had gained with their W25 and W125 Grand Prix cars. They had conquered all before them, receiving a serious challenge only from another German make, Auto Union, the designer of which was former Daimler-Benz employee, Dr Ferdinand Porsche.

Into this completely new design of chassis went a rear suspension that was very similar to that of the W24 that preceded it, being of the De Dion type, using large-diameter coil springs as a springing medium. The front suspension now consisted of unequal length upper and lower wishbones, again using coil springs, and lever-arm type dampers were mounted at both front and rear.

For braking, there was a twin-circuit hydraulic brake system with two master cylinders, one for the front and one for the rear brakes. The brake drums themselves were ventilated, which helped in cooling them as they slowed the huge bulk of the Grosser Mercedes. They also featured vacuum-servo assistance.

The steering system was by worm and nut and the car could be ordered in both left and right-hand drive. There was a central lubrication system in order to keep all the necessary joints well furnished with grease. A Maybach overdrive was fitted behind the four-speed gearbox in the pre-production cars but in December 1937 the factory confided by internal memo that a five-speed and reverse gearbox would be developed if demand for the new car was high enough. It was.

Adolf Hitler's motorcade makes its way through Vienna during his visit to the Austrian capital after the Anschluss in 1938. Hitler is riding in one of the new Mercedes-Benz Typ W150 Grosser 770s. (*Historic Military Press*)

The engine of the new W150 was further developed from that which had powered the W07 Grosser to become the Typ M150 design that went into the new Grosser Mercedes. This entailed redesigning parts of the new crankcase, as well as the mountings themselves being of a new design. The connecting rods, head gasket and flywheel were also new and the pistons now had just two plain and one oil scraper ring. A feature that was introduced on the W150 was sodium-filled valves, to help cool them. This would become a common feature of highly stressed aero engines.

Bore and stroke remained the same as the previous W07 engine, 95 × 135mm. There was a new crankshaft that ran in nine plain bearings, and the camshaft, also mounted in nine bearings, drove a new fuel pump, as well as the valves, via pushrods Essentially, although the supercharger was to a new design, it still used the same lobes as had been used in the W07. Power for this 7,665cc engine was given as 155 when unsupercharged, 230 when the accelerator pedal was fully pushed down and the supercharger cut in. Top speed was quoted by the factory as being 170kph but only 80kph for the few armoured, and therefore heavier versions, which were built for the Führer. This was mainly due to the construction of the bulletproof tyres, which each took two strong men to lift!

The Bosch starter motor was uprated to 3.0hp from 2.8 in the W07 and the distributor and magneto ignition, again using two plugs per cylinder, was very similar to that used on the previous Grosser Mercedes. Now, only two, as against three, oil pumps were needed for the new engine. There was a 195-litre fuel tank (the Grosser usually gave between 4 to 7mpg), and the now slightly slanted-back radiator was still an extremely elaborate affair of hand-cut square section tubes cut and soldered together, without a separate shell. It operated with a thermostat to give the correct temperature for the 535kg engine. As Hitler spent quite a lot of time in the Obersalzberg region, which has especially cold temperatures in the winter, two of Hitler's W150 Grossers were fitted with radiators made by Behr, due to temperature problems while running in these intemperate climes.

Hitler in Vienna during March 1938. (Bundesarchiv, Bild 146-1972-028-14/CC-BY-SA)

There were no fewer than four designs for the instrument panel, two of them of a rectangular design and two of them elliptical. They carried very much the same instrumentation as the W07 Grosser design.

Where bodywork was concerned, it would be provided by the body plant at Sindelfingen only. Either Pullman Limousine (Innenlinker) or open bodywork (Offener Tourenwagen) would be provided by the Sindelfingen factory. The pre-series car featured Zeiss headlights, as on the previous W07 design, but the production versions used Bosch headlights. The fuel system gave trouble in the early cars but this was swiftly rectified.[2]

The cars supplied to the Reich Chancellery were distinguished by having a flashing red headlight on the left side and a searchlight on the passenger side.

When compared to the old W07 Grosser, which had first emerged in 1930, it can clearly be seen from a comparison of the side views how much more 'modern' was the Typ W150 Grosser than the previous Typ W07 in looks. For a start, the radiator of the W150 was sloped slightly backwards, when compared to the upright type of the Typ W07. Streamlining was in vogue now. The front fenders were of a more sweeping design than that employed on the W07 and the front doors had their shut faces at the front much more swept back than the doors of the W07, where that line was upright. Moving further back along the car, the rear fenders are also much more swept back than those of the W07 and the trunk is now shapely, being incorporated into the rear of the W150, whereas the W07 had basically an extra luggage trunk, bolted to the back of the bodywork.

The W150 also sat nearer to the ground, further revealing its sleekness over that of the W07, which stood in a far more upright posture than did the then-new W150. Both cars carried two spare wheels alongside the hood, whose sides (and sometimes the top also) were louvred on both cars, but while the W07's spare wheels sat naked and exposed to the elements, the W150's had metal covers.

Inside both cars, in the Offener Tourenwagen and Pullman Limousine bodywork were three rows of seats. While the front seats of the W07 were of the bench type, the W150 had separate seats for the driver and passenger. The second row of seats were two individual ones on both cars and the third-row seats could accommodate three people side by side. The long wheelbases provided plenty of legroom for the passengers. Both cars were true seven seaters, ideal for the parades that Hitler and the Nazis used them for.

The weight of the complete car, depending on what type of bodywork was fitted, was between 3,400 to 3,900kg, which equated to some 7,480 to 8,360lb, approximately 3.7 to nearly 4.2 tons. Lightness was not a particular concern for the designers of the Grosser Mercedes. The weight of the armoured W150 Grosser

770s in Offener Tourenwagen form was some 4,100–4,320kg (9,020–9,504lb), with a payload of 500–650kg (1,100–1,430lb, six to seven people).[3]

The armoured Aktion P programme should be mentioned. By 1939, Erich Kempka, Hitler's chauffeur, was so concerned about the safety of his boss that he investigated the possibility of Daimler-Benz making a special armoured version of the W150 Grosser. Kempka suggested to Hitler that he should have his cars armoured against an attack that might (almost certainly!) kill him, after the attack that had killed Reinhard Heydrich, the acting Reich protector of Bohemia and Moravia in Czechoslovakia in 1942. However, Hitler steadfastly refused this until, as Kempka recounted:

> When the opportunity presented itself I suggested he should have a bullet-proof car built for himself. He turned this idea down at once. His life was in no danger from the German people! Even foreign powers were hardly likely to try to assassinate him! He was convinced that it was known abroad how much he was needed for the development of Europe.
>
> I was taken by surprise when war came. As head of the Führer's motor pool I was not at all prepared for it. Now the idea of the bullet-proof car began to dominate my thinking day and night. Despite Hitler's refusal to have one, in 1939 I had an open-topped example built, on my own initiative. Apart from the armour plating it was no different to any of the related types. I applied to Martin Bormann, who was in charge of the motor pool budget, for finance, but he declined to foot the bill since he knew that Hitler considered armour unnecessary. Thus I was forced to seek donations from wealthy friends to pay for the completed vehicle.
>
> On 8 November 1939 at the Bürgerbräukeller in Munich an attempt was made to assassinate Hitler. This provided me with the excuse to draw his attention to the existence of my bullet-proof car. On the drive from Berlin Anhalter station to the Reich Chancellery I managed to obtain his agreement at least to look at it. Once in the Chancellery I had the new vehicle driven to the portico. Hitler looked it over with great satisfaction while I explained to him the strength of the armour. The windshields were of 45-mm multi-layer glass (40 millimetres (1.6 in) glass windows elsewhere), the side armour 3.5–4mm, 18 millimetres (0.71 in) steel armour plate in all metalwork surrounding the main passenger compartment, while the floor had 9–11mm plate as protection against land mines or bombs. The car was bullet proof against hand guns and explosives up to about half a kilogram of dynamite. 'In future I will use only this car, for I can never know when some idiot might throw another bomb in front of my vehicle,' Hitler remarked to Bormann with a smile. Bormann now

Accompanied by the German Foreign Minister, Joachim von Ribbentrop, British Prime Minister Neville Chamberlain is driven in one of Hitler's Mercedes to meet the German leader. It is believed that this photograph was taken during the second round of talks. On Thursday, 22 September 1938, Chamberlain flew from Heston, London, to Cologne-Bonn airport for a meeting with Hitler in the Rheinhotel Dreesen at Bad Godesberg near Bonn. This was the second of three trips to Germany that month that ultimately led to the Munich Agreement. He travelled in Lockheed 14 G-AFGN, which was flown by Eric Robinson. He returned to London on Saturday, 24 September. (*Historic Military Press*)

> had to pay for the vehicle. The boss was enthusiastic about my new bulletproof car. I was given orders to commission several more.[4]

This car was called the W150 Aktion P and weighed 4,100kg. Ten were built from 1940 to 1943, and they were also equipped with 19in armoured steel wheels and bulletproof twenty-chamber tyres. The fenders/wings were made of aluminium to reduce weight; maximum speed was now 80kph (50mph).

Other compartments were for three machine pistols. There were added vents to the top and side of the hood/bonnet, presumably because the engine tended to run hotter than in a 'normal' Grosser, having to move the extra weight along and particularly when moving slowly in a parade, and there were two strengthened hinges on the doors and four more vents in the scuttle.

Kempka also wrote that:

> Vehicles with special bodywork were always under construction under my supervision, as gifts from Hitler to foreign Heads of State. Repeatedly I would visit the factory to check how assembly was proceeding and ensure that all extra features were being fitted. Only rarely did I have more than a day for this task, and I would often have to work through the night to keep abreast of my other duties. Hitler required me to keep him permanently informed about the progress of these cars at the works, just as he interested himself especially in all technical matters and innovations.[5]

It is important to note here that these top-of-the-line Mercedes-Benz W150 limousines were only supplied new to Hitler for him and his highest ministers to use. Unlike Rolls-Royce or Cadillac, or any other maker, they were never sold to anyone else. All production was specially built for Hitler's Reich Chancellery. Some cars were given, as can be seen from Kempka's words, by Hitler to other dignitaries in countries the Führer was close to, but no one other than Hitler could go to Mercedes-Benz and buy a W150 from the factory.

Two cars were delivered to Hitler's occupation force in Norway, presumably for the heads of the government there, and Hitler gave a car each to Field Marshal Mannerheim of Finland and General Francisco Franco, the dictator of Spain.

Chamberlain is driven in one of Hitler's Mercedes to meet the German leader. accompanied by von Ribbentrop. (*Historic Military Press*)

Hitler's own Grosser cars were nearly all Offener Tourenwagens as he believed that it was important for the German populace to be able to see him clearly when he was in a motorcade for ceremonial occasions. To this end, he had a 'standing platform' built into all his cars, which consisted of a platform in the passenger compartment as he always sat in the front, except when accompanying visiting dignitaries.

Jakob Werlin had now achieved such success as the go-to man between Hitler and Mercedes that he was made a director of the company in March 1938.

By the time of the W150 Grosser's introduction in 1938, the world's makers of luxury cars had been decimated. Cadillac were still producing their V16 but sales had fallen to only a trickle by 1938. A total of 315 were sold in 1938, but only 138 in 1939, their last year of production.

Rolls-Royce were still in business and had one of the few cars that could compete with the W150 Grosser, the Phantom III, introduced in 1936.

Adolf Hitler, in one of the Reich Chancellery motor pool's 1938/39 Mercedes-Benz TypW150 Offener Tourenwagens in Klaipėda, a port city in Lithuania, on 22 March 1939. (*Polish National Archives*)

The Phantom III had a V12 engine, very similar in cubic capacity to the Mercedes-Benz, of 7,338cc. The valve gear was pushrod operated from a single camshaft in the valley of the vee, and by 1938 it was using solid tappets instead of the previous hydraulic tappets, which had caused problems. Like the Mercedes, it used twin plugs per cylinder. As in all Rolls-Royces, performance figures are hard to discover, but it probably put out some 180hp. One car was tested by *The Autocar* magazine in England and was timed as having a top speed of over 87mph, no match for the Grosser's 101mph.

By this time, Rolls-Royce had switched to an independent front suspension via coil springs, although the semi-elliptic springs of the rear suspension were a carry-over from the Phantom II. There was a four-speed and reverse gearbox and four-wheel, Servo-assisted, mechanically operated drum brakes to assist in the accelerating and braking of this 7,700lb car. The chassis had one-shot chassis

(This page and following). Adolf Hitler's Mercedes-Benz W150 Grosser 770 leads a parade held in Berlin on 6 July 1940, following his forces' victory in the West. The car he is in was one that he used often from 1938 on. (*Polish National Archives*)

lubrication and on-board jacking. In its short life, the four years before war stopped production, 727 cars were built and sold.

Something that is important to point out is that, unlike Rolls-Royce, Packard, Cadillac models, the 'Grosser' 770K was unavailable for sale to anyone except the Reich Chancellery. They were unavailable to even the richest people of the world.

The period 1938–40 saw Hitler take part in parades that marked the very height of his power. Once he had annexed Austria and reclaimed the Sudetenland and Czechoslovakia, each followed by a triumphant parade through Berlin, his next greatest achievement was in directing the Wehrmacht and Luftwaffe to take first of all Poland in September, 1939, and then France, Belgium and the low countries, which they did in a Blitzkrieg from 10 May to 22 June 1940.[6]

This was followed in July by yet another triumphal procession through Berlin with cheering crowds on either side of his Mercedes-Benz Grosser W150 through flower-strewn streets. At that moment, he must have felt as if he were the king of the world.

In March 1942, Hitler told the board of Mercedes-Benz, through an intermediary, that due to war conditions, it was pointless to expend effort on the design of new cars and so all efforts in this direction ceased.

There was also a factory programme in which twenty 540Ks were used to provide even more vehicles for the Aktion P programme of armoured passenger cars. These were, apparently, for the use of Hitler's 'senior management', and were ordered in 1942. This involved eighteen 540K Innenlinkers being confiscated (one

One of the Mercedes-Benz 540K Innenlinker Aktion P cars.

Hitler (standing on the left in the first car) during a parade in Berlin on 20 April 1939. (*Polish National Archives*)

wonders at their owners' reaction to this) and two new ones built, the older ones having their original bodies removed at the factory and presumably scrapped. A new armoured body was then refitted to the old chassis, which in the meantime had been refurbished by the factory. The windshield was of 35mm safety glass and the other windows of 30mm safety glass. The roof, floor and sides were of 2.3mm steel.

There is certainly one extant, unrestored in the USA, that had belonged first of all to the newly formed Volkswagen programme and was delivered to them in June 1939. Hitler *may* have used it in his visit to the factory in Wolfsburg (then Fallersleben) in July 1939, although this seems doubtful as he would probably have travelled there in one of his W150 Grosser 770s. There are at least two other Aktion P Mercedes-Benz 540Ks still in existence.[7]

Mention of the Volkswagen, that pet project of Hitler's 'Strength through Joy' programme of a car for the people, brings to mind that it would be remiss of this author not to point out that this 'Brainchild' of Ferdinand Porsche was definitely 'inspired' (if not outright copied) from Hans Ledwinka's Tatra T77, designed and built in Czechoslovakia prior to the advent of the Volkswagen, but with some misguided suspension ideas from Porsche thrown in. Nevertheless, after the Second World War, the Beetle went on to become one of the biggest-selling cars of all time, well and truly cementing the reputation of German engineering worldwide.

There had been an intention by Mercedes-Benz to replace the straight-eight-cylinder W150 design by a V12-engined car, designated the W148, and then the W157 before the beginning of the war in 1939, and Daimler-Benz was intent on designing a twelve-cylinder successor to the W150 Grosser 770.

The W148 used basically a W150 chassis with a 6-litre V12 engine, using overhead valves. This unsupercharged engine gave 170bhp at 3,600rpm and gave the prototype a maximum speed of 160kph. With a supercharger employed the engine developed 240bhp and the speed rose to 170kph.

The W157 was built on a shortened chassis and the prototype was timed at 190kph. Both cars were built as a few prototypes (perhaps six in all), but their development took far longer than expected and in March 1942 the project was cancelled.[8]

The Mercedes-Benz 770 F-Cabriolet presented to Gustav Mannerheim by Hitler at Mikkeli on 24 July 1942. It is often stated that the vehicle was a 75th birthday present to the Finnish leader, but in fact this came in the form of a trio of brand-new Steyr 1500 staff cars that were handed over on Mannerheim's actual birthday on 4 June that year. (*SA-Kuva*)

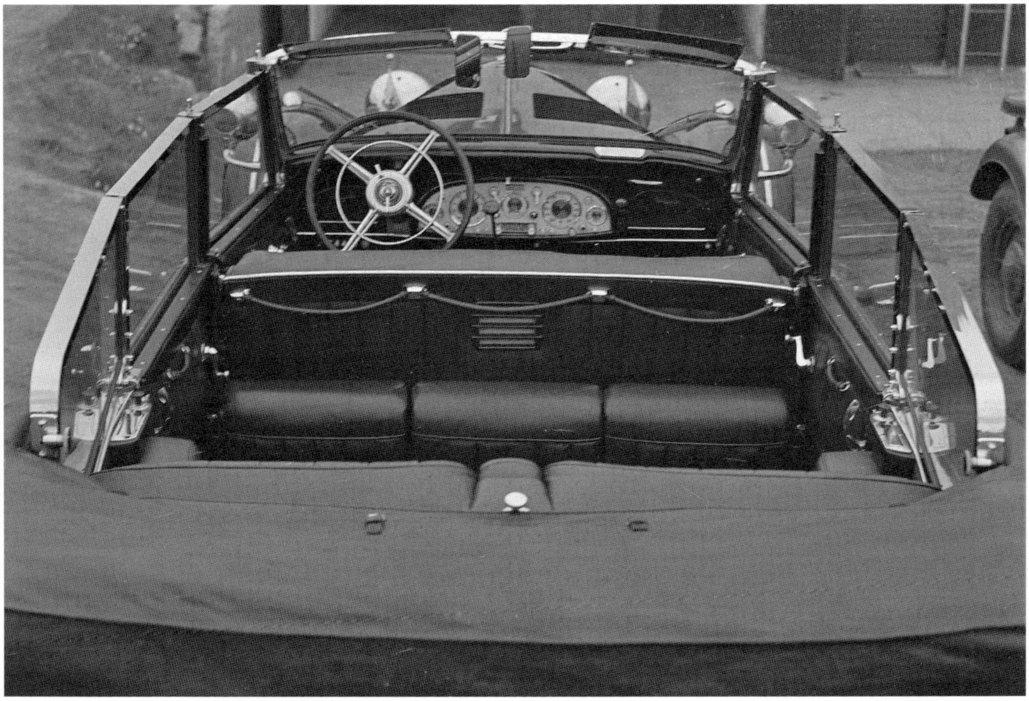

The interior of Mannerheim's Mercedes-Benz 770 F-Cabriolet at Mikkeli. (SA-Kuva)

The Mercedes-Benz Typ W150 Grosser 770 F-Cabriolet presented to Mannerheim at Mikkeli. The other two vehicles seen here include an earlier gift from Hitler to the Finnish leader (centre), a Steyr 1500 Staff car and Mannerheim's Packard. (*SA-Kuva*)

Mannerheim, on the right in his Mercedes-Benz 770, awaits Hitler's arrival at Immola airfield on a state visit to Finland to mark the leader's 75th birthday, on 4 June 1942. (SA-Kuva)

Field-Marshal Mannerheim of Finland with Hitler on a state visit to Finland, at Immola airfield in July 1942. Behind Hitler is his Mercedes-Benz W150 Grosser 770, (*SA-Kuva*)

Hitler getting into the Mercedes-Benz 770 at Immola. It is said that Hitler used this vehicle on two separate occasions – these being the journeys to and from Immola train station. (SA-Kuva)

Hitler in the Mercedes-Benz 770 at Immola. (SA-Kuva)

Hitler, in the Mercedes-Benz 770, arriving at the official train after a short journey from Immola. (SA-Kuva)

The W150 Grosser 770 was the greatest pre-war flagship of the company. A total of eighty-eight Mercedes-Benz W150 Grosser 770s were produced in the following years:

1938: 13
1939: 44
1940: 1
1941: 1
1942: 10
1943: 19

In 1938 and 1939, the price of an Offener Tourenwagen Grosser W150 770K, depending on fittings and accessories, was 45,000–47,000 Reichsmarks. For this price, in America, one could have bought sixteen Ford V8s. Hitler ordered ten W150s for the Reich Chancellery motor pool.

The Motor, a British magazine much favoured by the car trade, which carried a lot of advertising, tested a W150 Grosser Mercedes 770 in May, 1939, calling it the 'Super' Mercedes. This car was registered in Germany as IIIA-48003. Under the headline 'An Eight-seater Limousine Capable of Well Over 100 m.p.h. First Car of New Type with Engine of 7.7 litres Supercharged', the article stated that:

> One of the most striking exhibits at Earls Court last October and at other European motor shows since, has been the immense polished chassis of the 7.7-litre Super Mercedes. The first of the complete cars has just appeared in England and, as expected, it proves to be a vehicle of quite exceptional interest, capable of a maximum of well over 100 m.p.h. with eight-seater limousine coachwork.

This new Grosser Mercedes 770 had earned a place among the very top echelons of 'fine cars of international repute' said *The Motor*, and went on to give a very full description and driving impressions.

It was, said the article, a 'Giant in Disguise', quoting the Grosser's wheelbase being 12ft 8½in, the track as 5ft 3in in front and 5ft 4½in at the rear, and the overall length of the car as 20ft 6in. The height was 5ft 10¼in.

The Motor went on to say that: 'Although it is one of the largest, if not, indeed, the biggest car in production in the world at the present time, its size is to some extent disguised by carefully balanced proportions and it is not until it is seen alongside other large cars that its real dimensions are apparent.'

This, the article went on to say, gave the coach builders great scope for comfortably accommodating up to nine people within its capacious wheelbase, and that: 'Details of finish and equipment are entirely to owner's requirements. Interior fittings are silver-plated, and woodwork is polished ebony, with pewter stringing.'

Where the dashboard was concerned, *The Motor* described a typically German affair with all the instruments being laid out in a practical manner on a white panel where:

> A blue section on the revolution counter stretches from 2,500 to 3,500, and a red warning mark extends from 3,500 to 4,000 which seems not unreasonable on an eight-cylinder engine of 7.7 litres capacity. At the top of the panel is a strip-light indicator working in conjunction with a four-way tap to show the amount of petrol in the tank, the last section being red. There is little excuse for running short of fuel as the rear tank carries a main supply of 40 gallons, with another three gallons in reserve, and a separate tank, carried in the scuttle, holds a further four gallons for emergency use, with a gravity feed to the carburettor.

The article then described the ignition system of the engine. 'Dual ignition is provided, by coil and magneto, each cylinder having two sparking plugs, and a switch gives a choice of coil or magneto ignition or both.' It added that heating of the occupants was provided by ducts to the interior of the car, these being fed by warm air from the engine's cooling system.

Where the chassis was concerned, *The Motor* pointed out that it was obviously derived from experience gained by Mercedes with their Grand Prix cars, being constructed from oval tubing, welded together, and that the front suspension was independent at the front, using coil springs with parallel acting links, and, at the rear, again in the fashion of the racing cars, the use of a De Dion type of axle was similar to that used on those cars in the recent past.

About the Grosser's engine, *The Motor* waxed lyrical. 'The engine is, of course, magnificently finished and the spectacle under the bonnet is one to delight the eye of an enthusiast.' There then followed a technical description of the Grosser's supercharged straight-eight engine, with overhead valves, pointing out that: 'In accordance with the Mercedes system of optional supercharging, the Roots-type blower is mounted ahead of the carburetter and when the supercharger is in operation the carburetter is under pressure. Without the supercharger the engine develops 155 b.h.p., but when the accelerator is fully depressed to operate the clutch which brings the blower into action, the power is immediately stepped up and a power of no less than 230 b.h.p. is available.' The effect on acceleration was instantaneous, said *The Motor*, 'even though the car weighs 3 tons 12 cwt. unladen.' Mention was then made of 'the use of valve-seat inserts and sodium-cooled exhaust valves'.

'Particular interest attaches to the rear suspension,' said the article, it being composed of two large coil springs with the differential casing mounted to the frame, the weight of it all carried on two large tubular cross-members at the rear of the chassis. 'From here the drive is transmitted through swing axles, torque and braking stresses being taken by a triangulated tubular framework pivoted at the rear and amidships on another large tubular cross-member.'

The testers then went on to discuss just what the Grosser Mercedes was like to drive and said: 'In driving the car, one's first impression is of the ease of control, despite its great size and the additional disadvantage imposed by left-hand drive in English traffic.' The Grosser could, the article said, be ordered with either left or right-hand drive.

Even without power steering for such a large and heavy car, the writer went on to say: 'The steering requires three-and-a-quarter turns from lock to lock; which is by no means excessive and calls for no more effort than on many smaller cars. It is accurate and has good castor action; it is sensitive, so that one places the car confidently from the start, and it does not transmit shock.'

The Motor then went on to talk about the actual performance of the Grosser and gave figures showing that the car could accelerate from 0 to 50mph in 12.2 seconds and from 0 to 60mph in 17 seconds, no mean feat for a car weighing almost 4 tons, with passengers. The standing quarter mile without using the supercharger or forcing gear changes through took 21 seconds. Using the supercharger raised the terminal speed from 75 to 87mph.

Where maximum speed, tested at the old pre-war Brooklands circuit, was concerned, *The Motor* reported:

> Timed over a quarter of a mile the car clocked 100 m.p.h. with some ease, carrying four people; indeed, it was accelerating along the whole length of the Railway Straight at Brooklands. The speedometer is very nearly accurate, erring slightly on the side of slowness lower down the range, and the ultimate readings obtained suggest that the absolute maximum speed is in the region of 108 m.p.h., a truly impressive velocity for an eight-seater limousine weighing over 3½ tons.
>
> By way of contrast, it is equally fascinating to drive the car gently, making full use of the top gear of the 5-speed gearbox, which is an overdrive ratio. If the overdrive is engaged at 50 m.p.h. the engine speed drops immediately to 1,500 r.p.m., which is little more than a tick-over speed, and high cruising speeds are naturally maintained without any fuss. Moreover, there is quite a fair

> degree of flexibility in the overdrive ratio. There is synchromesh engagement for second, third, fourth and fifth speeds, and the change is easy, but should not be hurried.

The writer then went on to extoll the brakes, which he wrote, 'Are immensely powerful, giving results far superior to those obtained on commercial vehicles of similar weight, and fully comparable with those obtained on passenger cars of smaller size.' These brakes were hydraulically operated and had separate slave cylinders for each shoe, and a servo that relieved the pedal effort that would otherwise be needed. 'It is difficult,' the writer said, 'to find standards of comparison among other private vehicles.'

The article pointed out that where the coachwork was concerned, this included an open tourer, a smart convertible cabriolet for five persons and a large cabriolet to seat eight, and that: 'We did some fast travelling on winding roads and the general standard of handling and road holding is undoubtedly very good indeed. The absolutely rigidity of the tubular chassis is well reflected in the road-holding.' It added: 'The whole car gives an impression of considerable stability.'

On engine noise, *The Motor* stated: 'When ticking-over it is practically impossible to detect that the engine is running, either by sound or by feel. In normal use it is quiet although not absolutely silent. When the supercharger is engaged, of course, the characteristic Mercedes scream bursts out into full song, and the effect on loiterers holding the crown of the road is electric.'

The Motor added that every car had faults and that the front compartment suffered from excess engine heat, although this could probably be cured by extra insulation around the scuttle.

The article concluded with some slight criticism about the mounting of the differential casing on the frame, which: 'Places a premium on smoothness throughout the transmission. At present a certain amount of roughness and vibration is perceptible from the transmission, a point which can pass unnoticed with the orthodox type of axle. The final drive, too, is not completely silent, and this will no doubt receive attention.'[9]

Didier Charvet, who wrote for the French motoring magazine *Auto-Journal*, drove the Grosser W150 that was in the Henri Malartre Museum in France in 1965. He recorded that he was concerned about driving 'this monster of almost five tons' (this was an armoured Grosser). He pointed out that he and his crew were 'a little disappointed' as the car seemed to lack power.

After appreciating the clutch's easy pedal effort, Charvet went on to say that the handling of the gearbox was 'almost perfect'. After 10km, with the engine warmed up, his apprehensions were forgotten as, with the engine running smoothly now, he thought the acceleration was 'really brilliant!', and quickly forgot that the car was armoured.

The Grosser Mercedes was not pushed past 130kph, (about 80mph) due to the age of the tyres and also noting that the supercharger did not work. Charvet further reported how well the big car handled on small, winding roads and that it was as easy to handle as a (then current) Renault Dauphine. There was no vibration felt and the ride was very comfortable indeed.

Where fuel consumption of the Grosser Mercedes was concerned, this one reportedly returned over 50 litres for every 100km (about 6mpg), and the heater worked very well. Charvet finished the test by reporting that although some twenty-five-plus years had elapsed since this Mercedes was built, it still remained at a level that 'few cars of the sixties were able to reach'.[10]

Ever since the Treaty of Versailles was revoked by Hitler in 1935, the allies of the First World War had thought that they would be fighting Germany again, this time headed by Hitler. Steadily, watching Germany's rearmament, Britain, France, Italy and Russia also rearmed in the 1930s, although at a different pace to

One of Hitler's official cars, a Mercedes 770, on board the cargo ship *Nabob* in New York Harbour in 1959. The vehicle was being loaned for an exhibition. (*Courtesy of Buonasera*)

Germany, whose sights were set on lands to the east, as Hitler himself had declared earlier in "Mein Kampf" and in his speeches.

With the coming of the Second World War, when Britain and France declared war on Germany on 3 September, Germany went on to a war footing and political parades almost became a thing of the past. Indeed, the great Grosser Mercedes were not seen in public many more times, although a notable occasion was when Hitler led a parade through the streets of Berlin in July 1940 to celebrate Germany's victory over France in June.

From this time on, the great cars were used only sparingly and, indeed, when the end came in May 1945, many of them had been wrecked in bombing or artillery attacks, both at the Reich Motor Pool in Berlin and in the Mercedes factories. Whatever was left in Berlin at the Reich Motor Pool was gathered up by the Red Army and vanished behind the Iron Curtain, from where few cars have emerged since.

According to the Imperial Palace, this was a 1939 W150 Grosser 770 when in their collection in 2001. Chassis number 422396. (*Photo courtesy of the Imperial Palace, Las Vegas*)

One of the few exceptions emerged from Berchtesgaden, which the Americans occupied at the end of the war. At least one of Hitler's Grosser Mercedes was captured there, and shipped to America. Thought first of all to have been a car used by Goering, this was later on discovered to have been disinformation and its rightful identity as a car used by Hitler has been confirmed.

1938 Mercedes-Benz Typ W150 Grosser 770K specifications

Engine

Number of cylinders:	8
Bore × stroke:	95 × 135mm
Capacity:	7,665cc
Power:	155bhp, (Unsupercharged), 230bhp, (Supercharged). 3,200rpm
Compression ratio:	1:6.1
Firing order:	1-6-2-5-8-3-7-4
Gearbox:	4-speed plus overdrive, plus reverse

Chassis

Wheelbase:	3,880mm
Front track:	1,600mm
Rear track:	1,550mm
Weight-normal:	3,400–3,800kg
Weight-armoured:	3,700–4,500kg
Tyre size:	8.25 × 17
Max. Speed:	170kph
Max. Speed-armoured:	80kph
Fuel capacity:	195 litres

Production chassis numbers:

Late 1937: 189737 to 189744 (pre-series)
Then: 189744 to 189798. (397364 to 397367 were not built)
Then: 429311 to 429335. (439408 to 439432 were not built)
Then: 150006/0001 to 150006/0030. (last number produced appears to be 150006/025)

Note: Grossers in the Reich Chancellery Motor Pool, and used by Hitler. He commonly used the first ten cars listed below but was seen in others, listed beneath.

Without the Mercedes Archive being willing to give the information as to what registration/immatriculation numbers went with which chassis numbers, the list below is somewhat arbitrary. However, some cars are known by their chassis numbers and where so I have indicated them.

Reg/Immatric No: **1A-148461** (pre-series plate)
W150 Grosser 770
Chassis number:150003/0017
Engine number: 422396
Berlin registered.
Bodywork: Cabriolet F
Black.
Ordered: 30 September 1938
Ordered by: 'Führer and Chancellor of the Reich'
Delivered 27 July 1939
First armoured W150 for Hitler (according to Imperial Palace, Las Vegas)
Weight: 11,960lb

1940: 18/19 June: Munich. Mussolini visit.
6 July: Used by Hitler. Parade in Berlin celebrating the fall of France. Grosser. Convertible Limousine. Crossbar between front mudguards.
2000: Exhibited at Imperial Palace Casino, Las Vegas, USA.

Reg/Immac no: **1A-148764.**
W150. Grosser 770. Early/pre-series car.
Chassis number: Unknown
Bodywork: Offener Tourenwagen.
Black
Berlin registered
Ordered by: 'Führer and Chancellor of the Reich'
Crossbar between front mudguards

1938: 14/15 March: Vienna, Anschluss. Hitler used
1939: 23 March: Memel, Lithuania. Hitler
20 April: Hitler's car on his birthday parade

Reg/Immac no: **1A-148768**
W150 Grosser 770
Chassis number: 150006/0004

Bodywork: Offener Tourenwagen, (Convertible Limousine). Pre-series.
Black
Ordered by: 'Führer and Chancellor of the Reich'
Berlin registered.
Engine number: 189 789
Body number: 849 503
Berlin registered
Bodywork: Offener Tourenwagen (convertible limousine). Pre-series (Cabriolet B)
Aktion P, (high-protection panzerung, armour)
Crossbar between front mudguards

NOTE: This is probably also the car that was later registered 1A-103708, a number previously used on a Mercedes-Benz W24 also used by Hitler. That car was probably returned to the factory and the registration/immatriculation number used on the new W150. It was exhibited at the Musée de l'Automobile Henri Malartre, Rochetaillée, France.

W150 Grosser 770. Armoured

1938: February: Berlin Motor Show exhibit. Returned to Daimler-Benz for more work
26 March: Hitler. Konigsberg speech
20 April: Hitler's birthday parade
September: Nazi Party Rally, Nuremberg
15 September: Hitler used for meeting with Neville Chamberlain on his visit to Munich
1939: 20 April: Hitler used for birthday parade. Under den Linden
October: Used by Leutnant Commander Günther Prien, skipper of *U-47*, which penetrated Scapa Flow and sank the battleship *Royal Oak*
1954: 5 April: On display in Amsterdam

Restored. Black
Musée de l'Automobile Henri Malartre, Rochetaillée
2021: In existence

Reg/Immac. No: **1A- 148485**
W150 Grosser 770
Chassis number: Unknown
Berlin registered

Ordered by: 'Führer and Chancellor of the Reich'
Bodywork: Convertible Limousine. No vents under windshield
Black

1939: Presented to Hitler by Mercedes as a birthday present
20 April: Hitler. 50th birthday parade
1 May: Hitler. May day parade, Berlin
24 August: Hitler at Tempelhof Airport

Reg/Immac no: **1A-148599**
W150 Grosser 770
Chassis number **150000?**
Bodywork: Pullman Limousine. Coach (body?) number?
Black
Armoured

Ordered by: 'Führer and Chancellor of the Reich'
Delivered to the Ministry of Foreign Affairs
1940: Used to transport Foreign Minister Molotov during his visit to Germany

Reg/Immac no: **1A-148655**
W150 Grosser 770
Chassis number: Unknown
Bodywork: Armoured convertible limousine
Black
Berlin registered
Ordered by: 'Führer and Chancellor of the Reich'
Cooling slots on top of bonnet

1940: 21 November: Vienna. Hitler's arrival at Castle Belvedere

Reg/Immac no: **1A-148696**
W150 Grosser 770
Chassis number **150006/0003**
Bodywork: Pullman Limousine. Coach (body?) number **200787**
Black
Ordered by: 'Führer and Chancellor of the Reich'
Delivered 2 February 1943

1944: 15 March: Interview with Admiral Horthy at Klessheim Palace, Salzburg
1945: Seized at Berchtesgaden. Registered as: **Z96 501**
To France. 1945: At Berghof. Captured. Given by General Jacques Leclerc to General Charles de Gaulle. He gave it to the French Army Museum
Exhibited to raise money by 'Victoire', a French army association, which helped prisoners of war
1947: Shipped to USA
1949: Sold to a collector in Philadelphia

Reg/Immatric No: **1Av-148697** (pre-series plate)
W150 Grosser 770

1940: 8 July: Delivered.

Bodywork: Armoured Offener Tourenwagen
Berlin registered
Black
Cooling slots on top of bonnet. No guards behind front bumper.
Chassis number: **429334**
Order # 366 986. (3 November 1939)

1940: 8 July: Delivered to 'Führer and Chancellor of the Reich'
19 July: Berlin. Reichstag session. Kroll Opera House
1941: 10 September: Hitler to Marienbad to visit Admiral Horthy of Hungary
28 November: Hitler attended funeral of Werner Molders of the Luftwaffe
1942: 15 March: Hitler to the Zeughaus, Berlin
1943: March: Heroes Memorial day. Used by Hitler
19 April: Back to Mercedes-Benz 'for repairs'
15 September: Delivered back to the Reich Chancellery
4/5 May: Captured by Lance Corporal Joe Azzara, 20th Armoured Division, USA, at Berchtesgaden. Engine damaged, conrod broken. Another engine, from order number 399902, replaced the original
1945: 8 August: To New York

Stored 1947–56
Sold to car dealer R.J. Rumble
Re-registered as 1052-M
Sold to H.J. O'Connell
Restored
Sold to Claude Pratt

1971: In Canadian War Museum. Reg: WL-148697
1982: Shown to have been a Hitler used car. Ludwig Kosche

Reg/Immatric No: **IIB-215190**
W150 Grosser 770K
Chassis number: Unknown
Bodywork: Offener Tourenwagen. Armoured
Black
Munich registered
Ordered by: 'Führer and Chancellor of the Reich'
Hitler used

Reg/Immatric No: **IIB-215189**
W150 Grosser 770
Chassis number: Unknown
Bodywork: Offener Tourenwagen
Black
Munich registered
Ordered by: 'Führer and Chancellor of the Reich'
Hitler used

Reg/Immatric No: **IIB-215043**
W150 Grosser 770
Chassis number: Unknown
Bodywork: Offener Tourenwagen
Black
Munich registered
Ordered by: 'Führer and Chancellor of the Reich'
Hitler used

Other W150 Grossers used by the German government

Reg/Immac no: **1A-148656**
W150. Grosser 770
NOTE: This MAY be Chassis number: **150006/0019**
Bodywork: Armoured Pullman limousine
Black
Sindelfingen. Delivery?
Berlin registered
Used by Hitler

1940: 19 July: Berlin Kroll opera House: Hitler addresses the Reichstag about victory in France

Reg/Immac no: **1A-148699**
W150 Grosser 770K
Chassis number: Unknown
Bodywork: Armoured Pullman limousine
Black.
Berlin registered

1940: 12 November: Molotov visit, Berlin

Reg/Immac no: **11B-170124**
W150 Grosser 770
Chassis number: Unknown
Bodywork: Offener Tourenwagen
Black
Munich registered
Used by Hitler
Perhaps the car used by Hitler when he welcomed Mussolini after his German Fallschirmjäger aided his escape from Allied captivity in 1944

Reg/Immatric No: **IIIA-0037**. Stuttgart trade plate
W150 Grosser 770
Chassis number: Unknown
Bodywork: Offener Tourenwagen
Black
On test with Mercedes-Benz
This may also be:

Reg/Immatric No: **IIIA-48008**
W150 Grosser 770
Registered in Stuttgart
Chassis number: Unknown
Offener Tourenwagen
Black
Demonstrator/test car
Tested by *The Motor* magazine in England, 23 May 1939
Given to Arthur Seyss-Inquart, who governed the Netherlands during the war

1945: Captured by the Americans

Given to Prince Bernhard of the Netherlands. Reg. No: L-53826

Known chassis numbers

Reg/Immac no: **Unknown**
W150 Grosser 770
Chassis number **429311**
Bodywork: Cabriolet F
Black
1940
Rebodied by Sodomka, a Czech coachbuilder, after 1945. Used by Czech ministers

Reg/Immac no: **1A-485485/SS 02047**
W150 Grosser 770
Chassis number **429317**
Bodywork: Offener Tourenwagen
Black

1939: 20 June: Ordered by the Soennecken AG, Bonn
September: Order cancelled due to the outbreak of war

Note: At this point, the registration/immatriculation number was probably transferred to the car that was given by Hitler as a birthday present to Field Marshal Mannerheim of Finland, see below.

1941: 27 June: Ordered by Hitler's adjutancy. New body, painted dark blue
16 December: Given to Field Marshal Mannerheim of Finland. Chauffeur was Kauko Ranta
1942: 4 June: Finnish President Ryti collected Hitler from Immola airfield to visit Field Marshal Mannerheim
1947: 29 May: Sold to Costa Sverdrup, Sweden
September: Sold to Arne Gustafsson AB, car dealer, Eskilstuna
1948: Spring: Sold to Bildels AB
18 June: Sold to Christopher Janus, Chicago
1965: Sold to George Waterman, RI
Sold to Ed Jurist, Nyack, NY
Sold to Tom Barrett, AZ
1985: In San Diego

Reg/Immac no: **1A-485485**
W150 Grosser 770
Chassis number **Unknown**
Bodywork: Offener Tourenwagen
Black

1939: 20 April: Given to Hitler for his birthday

Reg/Immac no: **Unknown**
W150 Grosser 770
Chassis number **429328**
Bodywork: Cabriolet F/Offener Tourenwagen
Black
Delivered: 1940

Reg/Immatriculation No: **1A 235388**
Chassis number: **150006/0014**
W150 Grosser 770
Bodywork: Armoured Offener Tourenwagen
Black
Used by Hitler?
Restored

Chassis number: **150006/0011**
W150 Grosser 770
Bodywork: Armoured Offener Tourenwagen
Black
Delivered new to Reich Chancellery Motor Pool
Used by Hitler?

Chassis number: **150006/0009**
W150 Grosser 770
Bodywork: Offener Tourenwagen. One of ten.
Black
Used by Hitler?
Restored

Reg/Immatric No: **A-9293**
W150 Grosser 770
Chassis number **150006/0018**

Bodywork: Pullman limousine
Black

May 1945: In use by Quisling, Nazi head of Norway at the time

Dismantled

Chassis number: **150006/0023**
W150 Grosser 770
Bodywork: Cabriolet B
Black
Originally ordered for the Shah of Persia?
Used by Hitler
Restored

2021: In existence

NOTE: W150 chassis numbers **15006/24** and **15006/25** were at the factory on 2 March 1944 and were badly damaged in an air raid. Probably scrapped.

Chassis number: **150006/0030**
W150 Grosser 770
Bodywork: Pullman limousine
Black

Other Grossers

Reg/Immatric No: **1A-125521**
W150 Grosser 770K
Chassis number **unknown**
Bodywork: Pullman limousine
Delivered to Herman Goring
Blue

Reg/Immatric No: **1A-111**
W150 Grosser 770K
Chassis number **unknown**
Bodywork: Offener Tourenwagen
Black
Used by Josef Goebbels

Reg/Immatric No: **1A-611**
W150 Grosser 770K
Chassis number **Unknown**
Bodywork: Offener Tourenwagen
Black
Used by Joachim von Ribbentrop

Reg/Immatric No: **1A-617**
W150 Grosser 770K
Chassis number **Unknown**
Berlin registered
Bodywork: Offener Tourenwagen
Black
Used by Joachim von Ribbentrop

Chapter 7

Mercedes-Benz G4

The Mercedes G4 was an anomaly among the cars that Hitler used during his time as dictator of Germany. This was no luxury car to be used for parades, this was a six-wheeled heavy vehicle, built for the military. Hitler occasionally used them when he was inspecting military progress, such as in the campaigns against Poland and France, and, before the war, in the annexation of Austria. He also kept several at the Berghof, due to their ability, with six-wheeled

Hitler visits the Austrian city of Linz after the Anschluss, 13 March 1938. Hitler's journey through Austria became a triumphal tour that climaxed in Vienna on 15 March, when around 200,000 cheering German Austrians gathered around the Heldenplatz to hear him say that 'The oldest eastern province of the German people shall be, from this point on, the newest bastion of the German Reich.' (*Historic Military Press*)

Hitler enters Wildenau during a visit to the area in 1942. (*Polish National Archives*)

traction, to successfully get through the ice and snow that frequently blanketed that part of the world in the winter.

The G4 (known internally by Mercedes as the W31 from 1934 and the W131 from 1937), differed principally from earlier versions of Mercedes' six-wheeled military transport in using the eight-cylinder engine of 5.4 litres, which was similar to that used in the 540K and the W24 luxury Offener Tourenwagen, all six of which produced were used by the government for their officials, including Hitler.

In the version of the M24 engine fitted to the G4, the supercharger was omitted and thus the engine had a different front cover to that used by the engine in the W24 car. The Solex 40 MMOVS up-draught carburettor, now not having to cope with the pressurised air from a supercharger, was a much more simple affair than that used on the M24 engine and the inlet manifold and air cleaner were also of a different design. The first versions of the G4 had the exhaust manifold mounted within the confines of the bonnet but later versions copied the W07/W150 Grosser type in having two pipes protruding from the right-hand side of the bonnet, leading to the exhaust system located beneath the chassis. An electric fuel pump, to assist in starting from cold, was installed to help pump fuel through to the mechanical fuel pump, which commenced pumping fuel once the engine had started. With the engine running, overheating and fuel starvation were sometimes experienced when climbing steep gradients. If this happened, the mechanical fuel pump could sometimes help in restarting the engine, while the electric pump helped not at all.

The chassis of the G4 was a very simple ladder affair, made of channel-section side members, with three cross-braces, including an 'X'-type brace towards the middle of the chassis, just aft of the ZF four-speed gearbox, and a tube type cross brace above the rear axles, from which the leaf springs for the rear suspension were mounted. This cross brace also contained ball joints, from which were mounted the Komet More H2 dampers and torsion bars.

There were two leaf springs mounted on each side of the chassis at the rear, with the two live rear axles mounted between them. The torsion bars were installed to relieve the load on the rear springs. Both rear live axles were fitted with limited slip differential brakes on both rear axles and were mounted in bearings, located between the upper and lower springs, which allowed for some forward and backward motion. The rear half shafts carried universal joints at either end.

The beam axle in use at the front was mounted on leaf springs also. Incidentally, all six leaf springs could have the number of leaves specified when ordering, to allow for whatever load/bodywork the particular G4 was meant for. A torsion bar was mounted here, to locate the forward and backroad movement of the axle itself. Boge dampers were in use at the front, frame mounted.

Dual circuit hydraulically operated brakes, using two master cylinders, were both operated via a shaft to the brake pedal itself. One circuit was for the front brakes, the other for the rear. A Bosch-Dewandre servo gave power assistance to the drum brakes. There was a central lubrication system fitted and the handbrake worked on the front drum brakes only. Steering was by worm and nut.

The Daimler-Benz transfer gearbox, intended only for low range, gave one ratio for normal driving and one for off-road driving. It was combined with the ZF four-speed and reverse Aphon gearbox, all operated via single plate clutch but with a lever to select the normal four speeds, and another to select high or low in the transfer gearbox. Wheels were of 17in diameter and 7.5in wide. The G4 weighed some 3,500kg, 4.5 tons in daily use, and could only reach 67kph. Certainly the next

Following in Hitler's footsteps, other senior Nazi leaders made visits to Austria in the aftermath of the Anschluss. In this case it is Hermann Goering making his way through the streets of Vienna in an official Mercedes-Benz Typ W131/G4 on 26 March 1938.

Having arrived in a Mercedes-Benz TypW131/G4, Hitler is greeted by an officer in Poland in September 1939. (*Courtesy of Josef Gierse*)

step in the development of this heavy military vehicle would probably have been a half-track, using tracks at the rear for added grip, but the war ended before a G4 equipped like this could emanate from the Mercedes-Benz factory.

For bodywork, the G4s were usually 'Offener Tourenwagens' (open touring cars), while some were given saloon/sedan type bodywork, particularly those used as radio communication cars when in military service.[1]

By 1934, a black G4 was being tested across country. Registered IIA-19316, a Bavarian registration, it was used by the factory to find out its limits across rough, hilly countryside. Afterwards, it was used by Herman Goering, commander of the Luftwaffe. Later on, Goering also used another G4, registered in Berlin as IA-103727.

Erich Kempka, Hitler's chauffeur, wrote in his book about the G4s that Hitler used:

> It was always my pleasure to watch over the new vehicles as they were being manufactured. Under my supervision and in close cooperation with the Daimler- Benz factory not only were the well-known Führer-cars built but also cross-country vehicles for manoeuvres, later used for drives in the mountains and later still well proven during the war.

> On one occasion Hitler ordered me to place an experimental vehicle from Daimler-Benz at the disposal of the Berchtesgaden Mountain Rescue. It was to be used in the rescue of two mountaineers on the Watzmann. Only through the use of this vehicle could the men be saved. As a result of this success, other cars of the type were built and donated to the Mountain Rescue.[2]

Hitler used at least one G4 during his trip to Poland in October 1939 to observe how the campaign there was going. He was escorted by two more G4s, each machine-gun armed. In another G4, Hitler visited the Western Front on 26 December 1939. Several were kept as part of the collection of cars used by Hitler and his entourage at the Berghof, for use when weather conditions such as snow and ice prevented the use of a Grosser Mercedes.

From factory records, it would appear that some seventy-two G4s were produced.[3]

G-4 specification

Engine Type:	M24, less supercharger (Kompressor)
Cylinders:	Inline eight formation
Bore × stroke:	Either: 86 × 108 or 88 × 111mm
Displacement:	5,018/5,252/5,401cc
BHP at 3,400rpm:	100/110/115
Compression ratio:	5.6:1
Firing order:	1-3-6-8-4-2-7-5
Carburettor:	Solex updraft twin
Fuel pumps:	Mechanical Jumo Lv0 760a and two Electric 'Petrolift' pumps
Brakes:	Dual-circuit hydraulically actuated, with servo assistance for all six wheels
Wheelbase:	3,100 + 950mm
Front track:	1,620mm
Rear Track:	1,570mm
Weight:	3,450–3,890kg
Tire size:	7.50-17
Maximum speed:	67kph
Fuel consumption:	36 litres per 100km
Fuel capacity:	90 litres, including 8 litres reserve

G-4 Cross-country touring cars

Reg/Immac no: **11B-215043**. Grosser. W151. G4. Hitler used
Ordered by: 'Führer and Chancellor of the Reich'
Used at Hitler's retreat at the Berghof, Obersalzberg

Reg/Immac no: **11B-215190**. Grosser W151. G4. Armoured
Ordered by: 'Führer and Chancellor of the Reich'
Munich registered/kept. Hitler used

Reg/Immac no: **11B-215289**. Grosser. W151. G4
Hitler used
Ordered by: 'Führer and Chancellor of the Reich'

WH-32288
Hitler used

1938:	1 October: Hitler in Sudetenland, Czechoslovakia
	3 October: Hitler in Eger, CZ
	7 October: Hitler in Freudenthal, Sudetenland
	8 October: Hitler in Jagendorf, Sudetenland
	10 October: Hitler reviewed SS Totenkopf division in the Sudetenland
2005:	In Imperial Palace Collection, Nevada
2021:	With the Wheatcroft collection, Leicestershire

WH-32290 (W = Wehrmacht, H = Heer)
Hitler used

1938:	12 March: Linz, Austria
	13 March: Braunau. Hitler's birthplace. Michaelsbergstrasse 16
	14 March: Melk, Austria. Then to Vienna

WH-37826
Hitler used

1939: March: March into Brunn, CZ

WH-32292

WH-37925
Hitler used

1939: 16 March: Prague, Brunn

1A-100199 G4
Goering used.
21 September 1939: Poland

1940: Feb 29: Goering at Trier, Germany

1A-103727 G4
Goering used

1938: 26 March: Vienna
30 March: Bleiburg, Austria

1A-67510. G4
2015: In museum In France
re-registered as: RP-700203

1A-129155 G4
Fritz Todt

1Z-5750? G4
Hitler used

1936: 28 March: Cologne

11A-19316 G4
Goering. SS-41?

1934: On test

IIA-19350 G4 Chassis No: 105184
Berghof. Munich registered
Hitler used

1935: September. Meeting with von Fritsch. Wehrmacht military manoeuvres

IIA-19370 G4
Berghof. Munich registered
Hitler used

IIA-19570. G4
Hitler used
Berghof. Munich registered

IIA-22006 G4 Munich registered
Hitler used

1936: 6/2: Garmisch-Partenkirchen Winter Olympics

Chapter 8

How Many?

How many cars did Hitler have? Perhaps the real question should be, how many cars did Hitler have at his disposal? Let us take this year by year.

It appears that Hitler's first car was a green Selve 6/20, sometimes referred to as a '20CV', with a four-cylinder engine of 1,570cc, which Hitler's wealthy friends bought for him in 1920/21. There is a photograph extant of Hitler in a light-coloured Selve, which his friend 'Putzi' Hanfstaengl called 'the Rattling Monster'. It broke down quite often. In a second Selve, presumably in better condition, Hitler was chauffeured to his various speaking engagements by his girlfriend's brother, Ernst Haug, until Hitler's imprisonment for the Munich Putsch in early 1924.

When he came out of Landsberg Prison on 20 December 1924, Hitler was photographed by Heinrich Hoffman standing beside what appears to be a grey Benz 11/40, driven by Jakob Werlin, which had been sent to pick him up. It would appear that this car, sent to take Hitler back to his apartment, also acted as Werlin's demonstrator but it seems Hitler did not buy it, waiting until Helene Bechstein bought him a new Mercedes in early 1925.

As we have seen, while in prison, Hitler had corresponded with Jakob Werlin, the salesman for Benz in Munich at the time, about buying a Benz '11/40', as it is referred to in Hitler's letter to him in October 1924. However, the Benz 11/40 was discontinued at the end of 1924. There are then photos of Hitler in his first Mercedes in 1925, when Helene Bechstein bought Hitler his first supercharged Mercedes-Benz, a 15/70/100 open touring car. This had the licence plate number IIA-6629, registered in Munich, which was at the time Hitler and the Nazi party's base. Emil Maurice now took over chauffeuring duties from Ernst Haug and carried out that duty until Hitler dismissed him in 1928, after Maurice admitted having an affair with Hitler's half-niece, Geli Raubal.

The Mercedes 15/70/100 was also known as the 'Typ 400' and the internal designation at the factory was W836. According to the Mercedes Archive, a car with the engine number 48045 was not sold until 1926 so, with a lack of photographic evidence of just what car Hitler drove in 1925, we are at present at a loss to explain this conundrum. Reputedly, Mrs Bechstein paid 26,000 Reichsmarks for the car in 1925. If this is so, this car cannot have been the 1925 Benz 11/40 that Hitler

Standing beside his Mercedes 15/70/100, sometime after 1925, Hitler is seen here greeting friends. Rudolf Hess, his deputy, stands beside him.

discussed with Werlin while he was in Landsberg prison. That car was only 17,500 Reichsmarks when new.

By 1928, Julius Schreck had taken over the task of chauffeuring Hitler to and from engagements, and he held this position until his untimely death from meningitis in May 1936. Thereafter, Erich Kempka took over the job permanently. He had been employed by Hitler since 1932 in the motor pool and had shared chauffeuring duties with Schreck. Hitler was photographed in this 15/70/100 as late as September 1931. The Nazi Party was having a low time, financially, in the late 1920s, which may account for the fact that Hitler, or the party, does not appear to have bought another new Mercedes-Benz until at least 1930.

Judging by photographs, Hitler appears to have then used a Mercedes-Benz Typ W08 Nürburg 460 in the early 1930s. Strangely, he was also photographed in a Nürburg 500, with the same reg/immatriculation number, IIA-22006 in 1934. It is probable that as cars were traded in, their licence plate number could be transferred onto the newer car. Hitler's car was photographed again, from the side, in 1935 and it was definitely a Nürburg 500 in Berlin. Perhaps the same car as he was seen in the year before? There would probably have been a lot of them in the Reich Motor Pool. Hitler then moved into a series of even more imposing Mercedes-Benz, the Typ W07 'Grosser' Mercedes-Benz, from 1931 onwards. And then … the number

Adolf Hitler at a rally in September 1935. He is standing in one of the Reichchancellery Motor Pool's Mercedes-Benz Typ W08 Grosser 770s. This was one of the first 'Grossers' built. (*Polish National Archives*)

IIA-22006 appears again, this time on another W07 Grosser 770 in 1936. All these cars with this number were Offener Tourenwagens.

Hitler was involved in at least two car accidents, one in 1930 and one in 1931. The first car, his faithful 15/70/100, he later described as having damage only to its running board and fender, so that car was repaired. As we have seen, there is an insurance document that confirms this. Perhaps the second car from the accident of 1931 was badly damaged, written off by the tax authorities and the number transferred to another car?

Hitler was appointed Reich Chancellor (essentially the head of the government) in January 1933 and so from this date could use tax revenue to pay for his cars. Before this, he would have been reliant on his royalties from *Mein Kampf*. As this book sold over 5 million copies, it is easy to see that, probably by 1927–28, Hitler

HITLER IS INJURED IN AN AUTO ACCIDENT

German Fascist Runs Into Another Car—Foes Prepare to Meet 'Nazi' Attacks Next Year.

KYRITZ, Germany, Dec. 22 (AP).—Adolf Hitler, head of the German Fascists, suffered a broken finger today in an automobile accident. The car ahead of his skidded into a tree at the side of a country road not far from here, and Hitler's machine, in which General Von Epp was a passenger, struck the first car.

The Rev. Wenzel, who recently officiated at the marriage of Joseph Goebbels, National Socialist leader, received a broken nose. The driver of the other car was taken to a hospital with a fractured skull.

A report in the *New York Times* about Hitler's accident in 1931.

could have afforded the biggest and best cars that he wanted. He no longer needed loans or gifts from wealthy friends for such a purchase.

There is a photo extant showing Hitler still in his Mercedes-Benz 15/70/100 dated October 1931 and then the first photograph of him in the new Grosser Mercedes appears to be dated 10 November, so sometime in between the two dates, Hitler had bought (or perhaps the Nazi Party had bought for him), a new Grosser Mercedes, registered as IIA-19357, again Munich based.

Once established as Chancellor, Hitler's car collection (the Reich Motor Pool) grew quickly. By 1936, when Kempka became Hitler's personal chauffeur, there were at

Hitler arriving at an event on 13 August 1943. (*Polish National Archives*)

least eight W07 Grosser Typ 770 Mercedes plus the six W24s in the Reich Motor Pool, plus various Mercedes-Benz Nürburg 500s for the various ministers and SS guards. In 1936, for the opening of the Berlin Olympic Games, there were over forty official cars in use.

From 1936 until 1938, Hitler used several of the six W24s built. These were referred to in factory literature as 540L (L for long wheelbase/chassis). These were a development of the W07 Grosser but with the engine that went into the 540K roadsters, basically a supercharged 5.4-litre straight eight. By the time that these six cars were built and supplied to the Reich Motor Pool, Mercedes-Benz would have known that their new 7.7-litre Typ 770K W150 Grosser was on the way and would have told Hitler that it would be better for him to wait for the more modern, better-riding car.

As far as linking cars to Hitler via their registration plates (tags in the USA), I have counted eight W07 Grossers, three W24s and ten W150 Grossers used by him.

Chapter 9

Hitler's Campaigns

Hitler used the G-4 six-wheeled vehicles at his disposal to follow his troops on their campaigns in Poland, France and Russia. He also used one when he declared Anschluss with Austria, bringing Austria completely under German rule.

On 12 March 1938, following a brass band troop column, at 10 minutes to 4 in the afternoon, Hitler, in a Mercedes G-4 six-wheeled vehicle, was at his birthplace, Braunau am Inn. His father, a customs officer, had worked at this border crossing.

To mark the Anschluss with Austria, Hitler entered the country through the border town of Braunau am Inn, his birthplace, in a six-wheeled Mercedes-Benz Typ W131/G4. The original caption to this photograph states that it shows the German leader as he 'crosses the border into Austria'. (*Courtesy of H. Blair Howell*)

Hitler visits the Austrian city of Linz after the Anschluss, 13 March 1938, in a six-wheeled G-4. (*Historic Military Press*)

Hitler gave the command and the vehicles moved forward, taking him and his entourage into Austria. The way was lined with cheering crowds.

Through the villages of Tied and Wels, and through rolling countryside, passed the Führer's column and everywhere he went were cheering crowds, arms outstretched in the Nazi salute, 'Heil Hitlers' ringing out.[1]

At Linz it was the same story, although there must have been people who had not wanted to see this day and they stayed behind shuttered windows. It was eight o'clock when Hitler reached there. Linz was a city of some 120,000 people and it was reckoned that there were 100,000 people on the streets at this time.

Of course, Goebbels' propaganda department were there in force, filming the scenes of the Nazi leader's homecoming for later showing in the cinemas.

Hitler's visit to the city of Sankt Pölten after the Anschluss of Austria, 14 or 15 March 1938. (*Historic Military Press*)

Adolf Hitler in Brno, a city in the South Moravian Region of the Czech Republic, in March 1940, on the first anniversary of Bohemia and Moravia replacing Czechoslovakia and becoming part of the Third Reich. Hitler is once again seen in a Mercedes-Benz W131/G4 six wheeled military vehicle. (*Historic Military Press*)

Commentators went wild exclaiming on the mad scenes and even foreign news journalists agreed with the propaganda people about how many citizens were out in the streets to see Hitler arrive.

Hitler then decided that due to this welcome he would annex Austria outright to Germany and the next day, Monday, 14 March, he entered Vienna, the capital. From Linz, the Führer's entourage had travelled 120 miles, all along roads crammed with people who had turned out to watch his victorious advance. Flowers were strewn upon the road in front of his column but it had to stop and wait on several occasions, while the broken-down vehicles of General Fedor von Bock's army divisions were cleared out of the way by Hitler's SS men. Der Führer was not amused and consequently was not in a good mood when he entered the city.

He need not have worried. The crowds, although not as many as there had been in Linz, still gave him a spectacular welcome.

The SS report included: 'Hitler used a G-4 three-axle, cross country Mercedes, bearing the Wehrmacht licence plate WH-32290.'

In October, 1938, Hitler visited the newly reclaimed Sudetenland. With the backing of Goebbels' propaganda ministry paving the way for him, and surrounded, as usual, by the press and cameramen, he left Berlin on 2 October, together with Milch, Todd and Brauchitsch, to visit his newly claimed prize. Just as in Austria, he was cheered by adoring crowds in the villages of Asch and Eger and visited the abandoned Czech fortifications.

As his column of Mercedes G-4 six-wheeled cars, full of party officials and SS guards, made their way along the roads, Hitler must have been thinking and planning how he would annex the rest of Czechoslovakia, which he considered himself to be cheated of by the Munich agreement.[2]

We can do no better than to follow Hitler's campaign of taking Czechoslovakia, Operation Green, through the eyes of Erich Kempka, Hitler's chauffeur at the time, which he described in his book *I was Hitler's Chauffeur.* When writing of the opening up of Czechoslovakia in March 1939, Kempka wrote:

> On my instructions, my convoy – ten cross-country vehicles and cars, and four trucks – had proceeded to a small railway station on the Saxony–Czech border. Towards 0630 hrs Hitler left Berlin with the entourage in the Führer-train, and alighted at the Czech border, where my convoy of vehicles awaited, in a blizzard. I took my place at the wheel of the Führer's cross-country automobile. Hitler sat beside me and we led off the convoy.
>
> The customs officers at both frontiers appeared to have orders to allow us to pass. No attempt was made to stop us and the barriers were raised at our approach. The blizzard grew fiercer. We drove across Czechoslovakia at slow speed. The highways were slippery and one of our trucks went into a ditch. Its load was transferred at once to the other vehicles, and the truck was abandoned. We had no time to waste. Prague was reached at four that afternoon. Life in the venerable old city was going on as normal. Our passage through the streets went almost unnoticed. The snow storm continued.
>
> At the Hradčany Castle, seat of the Czech government, we were not expected, but quarters were arranged for us in a wing of the castle. A single company from an SS engineer battalion arrived, the remainder having been held up by the blizzard and icy roads. Towards 1700 hrs President Hácha, arriving by train from Berlin, came to the castle. He was astonished to see Hitler there waiting for him. He had not thought it possible for him to act so swiftly. The talks were resumed at once, treaties drafted and signed. Next day

the Czech Cabinet and a few military commanders arrived at the Hradčany. They were received and presented to Hitler.

This military occupation of Prague had been effected by an invasion force consisting of Hitler, his military escort and one company of an SS engineer battalion. This battalion had been formed in Dresden from a training unit under instruction and was so poorly armed that the men of the Führer's SS bodyguard had to lend them half their stock of machine pistols. Looking back on this situation today, it would have been no problem for the Czechs to have captured the lot of us. We had no heavy weapons and could have held out for only a few minutes.

On the afternoon of 17 March our convoy of vehicles left Prague. Heading north we passed the German occupation force heading for the Czech capital. At our original departure point on the frontier we boarded the special train for Vienna, where Hitler was expected.[3]

'Case White' was the name given by Hitler to the invasion of Poland, which began on 1 September 1939. Two days later, to Hitler's surprise, Britain and France declared war on Germany. Poland fell on 6 October.

Adolf Hitler and his SS driver, Erich Kempka, in a Mercedes W131 being greeted in Poland by jubilant German troops in September 1939. One source states that this image would have been taken in Warsaw on 5 October 1939, following Hitler's attendance at a victory parade there. (*Courtesy of Josef Gierse*)

Hitler visited the front several times in September; the 4th, 6th, 10th–13th and 15th. This beside a final trip to see victory in Warsaw on 5 October.

The Führersonderzug (leader's special train) was met at every stop by two columns of Mercedes G-4s, always available at a moment's notice for the Führer and at 9.30 a.m., on 4 September, the Führer's motor convoy moved out for the first tour of the front area from the station.

The Mercedes G-4s, in glossy beige with black mudguards, had their licence plates and insignia covered over and were not yet in the dull camouflage colours that they would shortly receive.

In the first column was Hitler's car, two Führerbegleitkommando (FBK) cars, one car for the aides, plus one more car for the then General, later Field Marshal, Wilhem Keitel, the chief of Oberkommando der Wehrmacht (OKW), and then even more aides. Besides Hitler in his car, and the driver Erich Kempka, there were several others and Heinz Linge, Hitler's valet, who carried a machine pistol. At this point, even Hitler carried a pistol.

Two more cars followed; they carried FBK men and Brückner, and had two machine guns mounted on each, together with several open cars. The SS, doing their duty as escort, were behind Hitler's car, and the RSD car brought up the rear.

Martin Bormann sat in the adjutant's car, with Major General Karl-Heinrich Bodenschatz, plus an SS aide of lower rank, and Heinrich Hoffmann, Hitler's personal/Reich photo reporter. A fifth car carried Keitel plus his adjutant, and the liaison officers of the Army and Navy. There was more transport, for people such as Dr Otto Dietrich, plus a reserve car, a petrol tanker and a field kitchen car.

Erwin Rommel, later to become famous as a commander in the desert, commanded the Führer's detachment. The FBK looked after the two cars and were preceded by a squad of motorcyclists and also by two armed reconnaissance vehicles. In the rear were five more motorcycle soldiers, followed by Rommel's car, even more motorcycle soldiers, an anti-aircraft platoon with their guns and a signal corps platoon.

Column K (for Kommandant) was followed five minutes later by the armed escort protecting Column M (for military). They had an anti-tank gun, then came the cars of Group 2, followed by another anti-tank gun and yet more of the signals platoon, which was accompanying Group 1.

At this time, German troops were crossing the Vistula at Topolno, and this was where the Führer first visited. Later on they went back to a new location where the Führersonderzug was waiting. They then travelled through Neustettin, Preussisch Friedland, Zempelburg, and Komierowo. Here, Hitler was briefed on the fighting situation by General Hans Günther von Kluge, Commander-in-Chief of the 4th Army.

The party left for Topolno after lunch, served from an army field kitchen. On the road, the convoy stopped after Polish soldiers had carried out an ambush on a hospital company, but the journey continued after security had been assured.

A lorry coming the other way, when the convoy was near to Crone, hit one of the anti-aircraft platoon cars. This was caused by the driver having been shot by a sniper. None of the Germans were to blame.

German troops, their aircraft identification sadly lacking, shot at the Fieseler Storch aircraft that had provided aerial reconnaissance for the convoy, while the travellers pressed on through Crone and Brzeźno to Pruszcz, Hitler then watched over the German troops crossing the Vistula at Topolno, and went back later to the same place to look at unfinished Polish bunkers. Bombs from Polish aircraft interrupted his inspection and so the convoy retreated through Vandsburg and Flatow to Pliessnitz.

On 6 September Hitler travelled to the front again, from Gross-Born, and then to Plewno. There, General Heinz Guderian commanded XIX Army Corps, and the trip following, to the bridge over the Vistula at Grudziądz, was carried out calmly.

On 10 September Hitler's motorised convoy visited Białaczów, after which his column drove to Końskie and to Masłów.

It was slow going for the convoy now as near the front there was a lot of military traffic, tanks, supplies and columns of infantry moving forward, and prisoners of war were seen constantly, going back to Germany. At Masłów, Hitler's Junkers Ju 52/3M and the group boarded and flew to Neudorf, where they arrived by car at 6.15 p.m. by car to Illnau. There, the Führersonderzug and von Ribbentrop's special train were waiting. On 11 September they made very much the same journey back to Bogusławice, west of Tomaszów, this time by aeroplane, and then by car to Wola before heading back to Illnau.

General von Blaskowitz was, on 12 September, just south of Lodz. He, General Ubex, who was north of Lodz, and General von Weichs at Bratoszewice, each briefed Hitler on the current situation in their area. This visit was carried out partly by air and partly by car. By this time, the column was based at Gogolin.

Three days later, Hitler and his entourage flew to Pawłosiów, arriving there at 10 a.m., but there was no convoy awaiting them. One hour later, it arrived, having driven for twenty-two hours, several vehicles having broken down. Hitler had already left, having assembled what road transport he could and went to look at troops crossing the San River, after which the column drove to Kraków later in the afternoon. Another trip was planned for 16 September, however this was postponed to the next day and then cancelled.

On 19 September Hitler visited Danzig, now Gdansk, where the 'Danzig Corridor' had provided the impetus for German resentment towards the new Poland after 1918. Hitler's military escort came to Zoppot, where Gauleiter Albert Forster met Hitler and his entourage. Reportedly, flowers were thrown and many people crowded on to the pavements and balconies and were to be seen at the windows.

There followed a journey to Westerplatte by minesweeper, and then by convoy to Gdingen via Zoppot. Then there was a trip to Dirschau on 22 September. Hitler watched Praga, a suburb of Warsaw, being bombarded by artillery and then moved on by road to Wyszków.

Hitler's next trip to Poland was very different. His Junkers took him to Warsaw on 5 October, to lead the victory parade, signifying the end of the campaign in Poland. His victorious generals, Milch, Brauchitsch, Rundstedt, Cochenhausen and Blaskowitz, met him and he was escorted into Warsaw by an Army detachment. The parade ground opposite to the Dutch embassy was chosen for the event and the two-and-a-half hour parade was made with due pomp and ceremony.[4]

After this campaign, Hitler's troops, supported by the navy, the Kriegsmarine, invaded and occupied Norway in early 1940, from 8 April to 10 June, forestalling an attempted occupation by the British.

Hitler's Wehrmacht and the Luftwaffe's next campaign (the Kriegsmarine had little to do with it) took place in France and the Low Countries, beginning on 10 May 1940. There, via a completely unexpected attack via the Ardennes forest, Germany scored a resounding success. In contrast to the more than four years of trench-fighting stalemate from 1914 to 1918, which had led to final defeat, Germany's forces forced France to sue for peace on 22 June, just six weeks after the start of the campaign. Once again, Hitler insisted on seeing the action from near the front on several occasions, again using the tough Mercedes G-4s.

On 10 May 1940 the FBK readied themselves to provide escort for the Führer, to go to where he could observe the fighting. The Graue Kolonnen (Grey Columns) were again assembled, made up of several Mercedes-Benz G-4s plus the usual SS escorts.

In Belgium and France, the German tanks and infantry moved forward so fast that Hitler's headquarters base was soon left behind. New tactics were required for the front groups and on 22 May, twelve days after the fighting had started, several front groups headed into Belgium in order to be available where and when called upon.

The front group led by Hauptmann Alfred Naehring (head of the 3rd Company) went to Aachen, Germany. Captain Otto von Blomberg, Chief of the 1st Company, led his front column to Charleville, Belgium; and Hauptmann Walther Barg, Chief

Hitler arriving at the Notre-Dame Cathedral in Strasbourg on 28 June 1940. (*Strasbourg Archives*)

of the Flak Battery, Front Group, went to Brûly-de-Pesche, near to Philippeville in southern Belgium. This was where the new Führer HQ was now positioned.

Hauptmann Naehring's Front Group (FG) was, on 29 May, told to move from Aachen to Brussels, meet Hitler's Junkers Ju 52/3m, and give military escort to the Grey Column. Blomberg's detachment went to the location between Tournai and Saint-Amand in Belgium. Hitler's intention was to tour the front in Flanders and Artois, with which he was familiar from his experiences in the First World War. The detachment's mission was to provide security where the Führer column would stop for the night of 1–2 June.

The battle for Lille had ended by the time the Kommandant had found and selected the Chateau de Brigode at Annappes as a stopover, just 6km east of Lille. Blomberg's unit moved there the next day.

Hitler flew from Odendorf to Brussels, arriving at 10 a.m. on 1 June 1940. There to meet him was von Bock, the sun shining down, and Hitler and his entourage boarded the Mercedes-Benz G-4s of the Gray Column and, with the protection of FG Naehring, the column drove towards the west through Ghent to Courtrai, Bissegem, Ypres, and Langemarck. There, Hitler stood in silence at the German First World War cemeteries at Poperinghe, Wervicq, Menin, Kemmel, and Lille, finally arriving at the Chateau de Brigode at 7.20 p.m.

The next day, at 10.30 a.m., the convoy went to Lille. There, Hitler and his staff climbed to the top of the citadel, where they viewed the city from high above. After this, Hitler's column drove off to Pont a Marcq, Avelin, Seclin, Carvin, Lens, Vimy Ridge, Neuville, Souchez, Loretto Heights, Arras, Douai, Bouchain, finally arriving at an airfield near to Cambrai in the early afternoon. Hitler had visited many of the places where he had been stationed in the First World War.[5]

Upon victory over France being declared, Hitler and his staff took once again to the Typ W150 Grosser 770s and led a flower-strewn parade through Berlin to celebrate the success over France.

Hitler used his train, *Amerika*, and his G-4s in the autumn to visit Mussolini in Italy, Franco in Spain and Pétain in Vichy France.

Hitler went once more to France, at the end of 1940, to inspect the defences that he had ordered emplaced along the French Channel coast.

Hitler visited his troops again on this occasion. On 16 December 1940, the FBK battalion was told of the Führer's train trip to tour the Channel coast and swiftly had its Mercedes-Benz G-4s ready to meet Hitler whenever he left the train.

The FBK were told to expect Hitler and they left their German bases in two columns on 23 December, no doubt some of them cursing that fact that they would be missing Christmas with their families. Hitler, together with his entourage, complete with the FBK escort, with their Mercedes-Benz G-4s, drove towards the west, in cold weather and over icy roads through Ardres and Guines to Rinxent, near to Marquise.

Hitler's group visited Cap Gris Nez on the Channel coast, from where it is only 21 miles across the Channel to the white cliffs of Dover. Here, Hitler inspected the artillery emplacement Grosser Kurfurst (Great Elector). This was one of the huge, concrete and steel emplacements, where German big guns could fire shells into south-east England.

That afternoon, Hitler's column drove south-west along the coast, and Hitler examined other long-distance batteries, They reached Boulogne at 3 p.m., and Hitler inspected the harbour. An hour later, the G-4s took Hitler and his staff to Wimereux station, not far from Boulogne.[6]

On Christmas Eve, Hitler's column visited Desvres, 20km east of Boulogne, so that he could visit Jagdgeschwader 3. This was a fighter gruppe and Hitler shared lunch with them. That afternoon, he and his entourage went back towards the

Hitler on a visit to an airfield on the Eastern Front, September 1941, during the early days of Operation Barbarossa. (*Polish National Archives*)

Channel coast. At 4.20 p.m., Oberleutnant Adolf Galland, the commander of Jagdgeschwader 26 'Schlageter' (later to become the general in command of the Luftwaffe's fighters), welcomed Hitler to his gruppe headquarters. Jagdgeschwader 26 was a highly successful group of 'Experten' (aces) with many victories between them (they were known by the British as the 'Abbeville Boys'). Hitler shared Christmas lunch with them the next day.

Hitler later told Goering that he thought the fighter pilots were 'scruffy' and Goering used this criticism of Hitler's when he later reprimanded Galland.[7]

After this, the Führer arrived at Metz, went for a short tour of the city and then boarded *Amerika* and arrived at Saarburg at 4 p.m.. There, he went by road, escorted by motorcycle troops, and inspected three infantry regiments. Afterwards, he climbed back on *Amerika*, and returned to Berlin, arriving there on 27 December.

The last great campaign which Hitler and the German forces embarked upon was the invasion of Russia on 22 June 1941. Hitler was profoundly interested in following the course of events during this campaign, and Erich Kempka remembered:

> Everybody has his good and bad side. Hitler made mistakes, but when he is accused today of lacking personal courage, that is unfounded. His entourage, led by Bormann and the generals, often criticised him for being too audacious for a Head of State: every day, for example, I drove Hitler myself to the front line to watch manoeuvres during the Polish campaign. Most of all I shall never forget a flight to Zaporozhye on the Dnieper, during the winter of 1942. The Russians were making a huge push to recapture the Donetz Basin – their main objective being the giant power station at Zaporozhye. We touched down at the western airport, the Russians having already seized back the eastern one with their tank spearhead. The generals begged Hitler in vain to get out of Zaporozhye, but he wanted to obtain a first-hand impression of the situation and so declined to leave. Not until the western airport came under attack from Rata fighters and he was satisfied that he had been sufficiently well informed during his four-day stay, and had ordered the necessary countermeasures, did Hitler give the order to leave. From Zaporozhye we flew to Vinniza near Zhitomir in the Ukraine, the summer FHQ on the Eastern Front, from where he proposed to visit endangered sectors of the front as and when problems arose.[8]

Notes and References

Chapter 1: Hitler's Early Life and Cars, 1889–1921

1. Sieg Heil = Hail Victor!
2. Kempka, Erich, *I was Hitler's Chauffeur*, Frontline Books, 2012.
3. Lehrer, Steven, *The Reich Chancellery and Führerbunker Complex: An Illustrated History of the Seat of the Nazi Regime*, McFarland, 2006.
4. Schwarzwaller, Wulf, *The Unknown Hitler, his Private Life and Fortune*, National Press Books, 1989.
5. Weber, Thomas, *Hitler's First War*, Oxford University Press, 2010.
6. The historyplace.com.
7. Weber, Thomas, *Hitler's First War*.
8. Ibid.
9. Schwarzwaller, Wulf, *The Unknown Hitler, his Private Life and Fortune*.
10. Ibid.
11. Ibid.
12. https://wikies.wiki/wiki/fr/Selve_Automobilwerke_A
13. Hanfstaengl, Putzi, *What I Remember of Hitler*, Macleans Press, 1957.
14. Schwarzwaller, Wulf, *The Unknown Hitler, his Private Life and Fortune*.
15. Kershaw, Ian, *Hitler: A Biography*, W.W. Norton and Co., 2008.
16. Toland, John, *Adolf Hitler*, Garden City, New York, 1976.

Chapter 2: Growth and Putsch, 1922–24

1. Hanfstaengl, Putzi, *What I Remember of Hitler*.
2. Weber, Thomas, *Hitler's First War*.
3. Dietrich, Otto, *With Hitler on the Road to Power*, Blurm, 2019.
4. Porsche, Ferry, *We at Porsche*, Doubleday, 1976.
5. Schwarzwaller, Wulf, *The Unknown Hitler, his Private Life and Fortune*.
6. Ibid.
7. Kershaw, Ian, *Hitler: A Biography*.
8. Hanfstaengl, Putzi, *What I Remember of Hitler*.
9. Kershaw, Ian, *Hitler: A Biography*.
10. Grehan, John, *The Hitler Assassination Attempts, The Plots, Places and People that Almost Changed History*, Frontline, Barnsley, 2022.
11. Kershaw, Ian, *Hitler: A Biography*.
12. Hanfstaengl, Putzi, *What I Remember of Hitler*.
13. Kershaw, Ian, *Hitler: A Biography*.
14. Schwarzwaller, Wulf, *The Unknown Hitler, his Private Life and Fortune*.
15. https://en.wikipedia.org/wiki/Jakob_Werlin.
16. Mercedes was a brand name of first of all Daimler, and then Daimler-Benz before those two manufacturers combined in 1924 to produce Mercedes-Benz cars and trucks

in 1926 and thereafter. It is possible that Wulf Schwarzwaller, who wrote this in *Adolf Hitler; his Private Life and Fortune*, did not realise that the predecessor to Mercedes-Benz was Benz and that this car was actually a Benz 11/40.
17. https://mercedes-benz-publicarchive.com/marsClassic/en/instance/ko/Mercedes-from-1926
18. Schwarzwaller, Wulf, *The Unknown Hitler, his Private Life and Fortune.*
19. Kershaw, Ian, *Hitler: A Biography.*
20. Schwarzwaller, Wulf, *The Unknown Hitler, his Private Life and Fortune.*

Chapter 3: The First Mercedes-Benz, 1925–29

1. https://en.wikipedia.org/wiki/Helene_Bechstein
2. Hanfstaengl, Putzi, *What I Remember of Hitler.*
3. https://mercedes-benz-publicarchive.com/marsClassic/en/instance/ko/Mercedes-from-1926-Mercedes-Benz-1570100-hp-from-1928-1570100-hp-Type-400.
4. Schwarzwaller, Wulf, *The Unknown Hitler, his Private Life and Fortune.*
5. Welch, David, *Hitler: Profile of a Dictator*, London, Routledge, 2001.
6. Kershaw, Ian, *Hitler: A Biography.*
7. Cooper, Matthew, *The German Army 1933–1945*, Scarborough House Paperback Division, 1990.
8. Schwarzwaller, Wulf, *The Unknown Hitler, his Private Life and Fortune.*
9. Brown, Eric, *Wings of the Luftwaffe*, London, McDonald & Jane's, 1977.
10. https://en.wikipedia.org/wiki/Jakob_Werlin
11. https://en.wikipedia.org/wiki/Mercedes_15/70/100_PS
12. Hamilton, Charles, *Leaders and Personalities of the Third Reich*, R. James Bender Publishing, 1984.
13. Weber, Thomas, *Hitler's First War.*
14. Kershaw, Ian, *Hitler: A Biography.*
15. https://en.wikipedia.org/wiki/Mercedes_15/70/100_PS
16. Venables, David, *Bentley, a Racing History*, Haynes Publishing, 2011.
17. Schwarzwaller, Wulf, *The Unknown Hitler, his Private Life and Fortune.*
18. Melin, Jan, *Mercedes-Benz 8, The Supercharged Cars of the 1930s, vol. 1*, Nordbook International Editions AB, 1985.

Chapter 4: Mercedes-Benz W07 Grosser 770, 1930–37

1. Melin, Jan, and Hernstrom, Sven, *Mercedes-Benz 8, The Supercharged Cars of the 1930s, vol. 2*, Gamla Bilsalongen AB, 2003.
2. Schwarzwaller, Wulf, *The Unknown Hitler, his Private Life and Fortune.*
3. Wagener, Otto, *Hitler: Memoirs of a Confidant*, Henry Ahby Turner, UP Yale, 1984.
4. Kershaw, Ian, *Hitler: A Biography.*
5. Hamilton, Charles, *Leaders and Personalities of the Third Reich.*
6. Weber, Thomas, *Hitler's First War.*
7. Melin, Jan, and Hernstrom, Sven, *Mercedes-Benz 8, The Supercharged Cars of the 1930s, vol. 2.*
8. Porsche, Ferry, *We at Porsche.*
9. Melin, Jan, and Hernstrom, Sven, *Mercedes-Benz 8, The Supercharged Cars of the 1930s, vol. 2 .*
10. Kempka, Erich, *I was Hitler's Chauffeur.*

11. Melin, Jan, and Hernstrom, Sven, *Mercedes-Benz 8, The Supercharged Cars of the 1930s, vol. 2.*
12. Melin, Jan, *Mercedes-Benz 8, The Supercharged Cars of the 1930s, vol. 1*, Nordbook International Editions AB, 1985.
13. Kempka, Erich, *I was Hitler's Chauffeur.*
14. *Auto Motor und Sport*, Verlag, 1931.
15. Taylor, Blaine, *Mercedes-Benz 770K Grosser Parade Car*, Schiffer Military History, 2010.
16. *New York Times*, 23 December 1931.
17. Taylor, Blaine, *Mercedes-Benz 770K Grosser Parade Car.*
18. Schwarzwaller, Wulf, *The Unknown Hitler, his Private Life and Fortune.*
19. Kershaw, Ian, *Hitler: A Biography.*
20. Schwarzwaller, Wulf, *Adolf Hitler; his Private Life and Fortune*, National Press Books, 1989.
21. Stargardt, Nicholas, *The German War, A Nation under Arms, 1939–45, Citizens and Soldiers*, Basic Books, 2015.

Chapter 5: Mercedes-Benz W24

1. Melin, Jan, and Hernstrom, Sven, *Mercedes-Benz 8, The Supercharged Cars of the 1930s, vol. 2.*
2. Melin, Jan, *Mercedes-Benz 8, The Supercharged Cars of the 1930s, vol. 1*, Nordbook International Editions AB, 1985.
3. Kempka, Erich, *I was Hitler's Chauffeur.*

Chapter 6: Mercedes-Benz 770 Grosser W150, 1938–44

1. Taylor, Blaine, *Mercedes-Benz 770K Grosser Parade Car.*
2. Melin, Jan, and Hernstrom, Sven, *Mercedes-Benz 8, The Supercharged Cars of the 1930s, vol. 2.*
3. Taylor, Blaine, *Mercedes-Benz 770K Grosser Parade Car.*
4. Kempka, Erich, *I was Hitler's Chauffeur.*
5. Ibid.
6. Stargardt, Nicholas, *The German War, A Nation under Arms, 1939–45, Citizens and Soldiers.*
7. Werner, Oswald, *Deutsche Autos 1920–1945, Band 2*, Motorbuch Verlag, 2001.
8. Melin, Jan, and Hernstrom, Sven, *Mercedes-Benz 8, The Supercharged Cars of the 1930s, vol. 2.*
9. *The Motor*, 23 May 1939. Road test of 1938 W150 Grosser 770.
10. *Auto Journal Magazine*, France, February 1965.

Chapter 7: Mercedes-Benz G4

1. Melin, Jan, and Hernstrom, Sven, *Mercedes-Benz 8, The Supercharged Cars of the 1930s, vol. 2.*
2. Kempka, Erich, *I was Hitler's Chauffeur.*
3. Taylor, Blaine, *Mercedes-Benz 770K Grosser Parade Car.*

Chapter 9: Hitler's Campaigns

1. Taylor, Blaine, *Mercedes-Benz G4 Cross-Country Touring Car*, Schiffer Military History, 2009.
2. Ibid.
3. Kempka, Erich, *I was Hitler's Chauffeur.*
4. Taylor, Blaine, *Mercedes-Benz G4 Cross-Country Touring Car.*
5. Stargardt, Nicholas, *The German War, A Nation under Arms, 1939–45, Citizens and Soldiers.*
6. Kempka, Erich, *I was Hitler's Chauffeur.*
7. Caldwell, Donald, *The JG26 War Diary, vol. one 1939–1942*, Grub Street, London, 1996.
8. Kempka, Erich, *I was Hitler's Chauffeur.*

Bibliography

Auto Journal magazine, France, February 1965.

Axis History.com forum, writer user name 'ucans', Hitler's Mercedes W07, W24 and W150, 2020.

Benz 11/40 hp, Mercedes-Benz-publicarchiv.com

Brown, Eric, *Wings of the Luftwaffe*, London, McDonald & Jane's, 1977.

Buchanan, Patrick J., *Churchill, Hitler and the Unnecessary War*, Three Rivers Press, 2008.

Caldwell, Donald, *The JG26 War Diary, vol. one 1939–1942*, Grub Street, London, 1996.

Cheetham, Craig, *Vintage Cars – The Finest Prewar Automobiles*, Grange Books, 2004.

Cooper, Matthew, *The German Army 1933–1945*, Scarborough House Paperback Division, 1990.

de Boer, Sjoerd, Traces of War, Tracesofwar.com, 2020.

Dietrich, Otto, *With Hitler on the Road to Power*, Blurm, 2019.

Grehan, John, *The Hitler Assassination Attempts, The Plots, Places and People that Almost Changed History*, Frontline, Barnsley, 2022.

Hamilton, Charles, *Leaders and Personalities of the Third Reich*, R. James Bender Publishing, 1984.

Hanfstaengl, Ernst, *Hitler, The Memoir of a Nazi Insider Who Turned against the Führer*, Arcade Publishing, 1957.

Hanfstaengl, Putzi, *What I Remember of Hitler*, Macleans Press, 1957.

Hawes, James, *The Shortest History of Germany*, Old Street Publishing, 2017.

Hoffman, Peter, *Hitler's Personal Security, Protecting the Führer*, New York, Da Capo Press, 1979.

Kempka, Erich, *I was Hitler's Chauffeur*, Frontline Books, 2012.

Kershaw, Ian, *Hitler: A Biography*, W.W. Norton and Co., 2008.

Lehrer, Steven, *The Reich Chancellery and Führerbunker Complex: An Illustrated History of the Seat of the Nazi Regime*, McFarland, 2006.

Lukacs, John, *June 1941 Hitler and Stalin*, published with assistance from the foundation established in memory of Amassa Stone Mather of the Class of 1907, Yale College, 2006.

MacMillan, Margaret, *The War That Ended Peace – The Road to 1914*, Random House, 2014.

Melin, Jan, *Mercedes-Benz 8, The Supercharged Cars of the 1930s, vol. 1*, Nordbook International Editions AB, 1985.

Melin, Jan, and Hernstrom, Sven, *Mercedes-Benz 8, The Supercharged Cars of the 1930s, vol. 2*, Gamla Bilsalongen AB, 2003.

Mercedes-model-k-1924-1930, Mercedes 500SEC.com, 2021.

Picknett, Lynn; Prince, Clive; Prior, Stephen; Brydon, Robert, *Friendly Fire*, Mainstream Publishing, 2004.

Porsche, Ferry, and Bentley, John, *We at Porsche*, Doubleday, England, 1976.

Robson, Graham, *The World's Most Powerful Cars*, Quintet Publishing Ltd, 1990.
Schwarzwaller, Wulf, *The Unknown Hitler, his Private Life and Fortune*, National Press Books, 1989.
Selve 10/40, forums.aaca.org. 2006.
Stargardt, Nicholas, *The German War, A Nation under Arms, 1939–45, Citizens and Soldiers*, Basic Books, 2015.
Taylor, Blaine, *Mercedes-Benz 770K Grosser Parade Car*, Schiffer Military History, 2010.
Taylor, Blaine, *Mercedes-Benz G4 Cross-Country Touring Car*, Schiffer Military History, 2009.
The Motor, 23 May 1939. Road test of 1938 W150 Grosser 770.
Toland, John, *Adolf Hitler*, Garden City, New York, 1976.
Venables, David, *Bentley, a Racing History*, Haynes Publishing, 2011.
Wagener, Otto, *Hitler: Memoirs of a Confidant*, Henry Ahby Turner, UP Yale, 1984. Weber, Thomas, *Hitler's First War*, Oxford University Press, 2010.
Welch, David, *Hitler: Profile of a Dictator*, London, Routledge, 2001.
Werlin Jakob, Wikipedia.
Werner, Oswald, *1886–1986 Mercedes-Benz Passenger Cars*, Motor-Verlag, Stuttgart, 1987.
Werner, Oswald, *Deutsche Autos 1920–1945, Band 2*, Motorbuch Verlag, 2001.

Index